The Nevis Company & Trust Laws

by
Adam Starchild

International Law and Taxation Publishers

London

The Nevis Company & Trust Laws

by
Adam Starchild

ISBN 1-893713-14-8

International Law & Taxation Publishers
London
http://www.internationallawandtaxationpublishers.com

Contents

Nevis: A Superior Asset Protection Haven

The "sovereign democratic federal state" of St. Christopher-Nevis (as its 1983 constitution ceremoniously describes it), has a governmental form and name almost bigger than its population (45,000), and total land area (267 sq. km.).

But this tiny West Indies island nation, known to the natives as "St. Kitts-Nevis," has become very big in certain exclusive international financial circles. That's because Nevis has no taxes, extremely user-friendly incorporation and trust laws, and an official attitude of hearty welcome to foreign offshore corporations and asset protection trusts.

In his second voyage to the New World in 1493, the year after Columbus discovered what was to become known as "America," (actually landing first at what is now the Dominican Republic), his explorations included two of the Leeward Islands. One of these he named (perhaps for a bit of ego gratification), St. Christopher, much later shortened to the current "St. Kitts."

It is reliably reported that when Columbus saw the smaller of the two islands, two miles south of St. Kitts, he was instantly impressed by the majestic volcanic mountain in its center, an almost perfect cone rising 3,232 feet, smothered in thick clouds. His diary indicates the intrepid Columbus was reminded of the snow-capped peaks of the Pyrenees, and so he named the island **Nieves**, the Spanish word for "snows."

Though Columbus claimed the islands for Spain, the first colonization was by the British in 1623 and 1628 respectively. In fact these islands became the mother British colony in the Caribbean, the launching pad for other settlements in Antiqua, Barbuda, Tortola, and Monserrat. The French arrived a few years later, inexplicably bringing a bunch of monkeys with them, and they (the French, not the monkeys) also used the islands as a starting point for their West Indian colonial designs in Martinique, Guadeloupe, St. Martin, St. Barts, La Desirade, and Les Saintes.

Located 225 miles east of Puerto Rico and about 1,200 miles south of Miami, until the islands September 19, 1983 declaration of independence, both were British colonies.

The islands are now a member of the Commonwealth of Nations and recognize as nominal head of state, Queen Elizabeth II, who appoints a local Governor General. The elected unicameral Parliament sits in the capital of Basseterre on St. Kitts (population 35,000), but Nevis (10,000) has its own Island Assembly as well, and retains the constitutional right of secession from St. Kitts. Now and again newspapers in Nevis (pronounced **NEE**-vis) issue heated editorial demands for separation, but if it happens, it will be without shots being fired, other than a few verbal salvos.

The tiny 2-island nation is a member of the United Nations, the Organization of American States (OAS) and is an associated Commonwealth participating state of the European Union (EU). It is also a member of the Caribbean Community (CARICOM) economic and trading group, along with fourteen other area nations including the Bahamas, Bermuda and Belize.

Although it was formerly a member of the British sterling bloc, the country's currency is now the Eastern Caribbean dollar used by several CARICOM nations, pegged to the United States dollar at a rate hovering around EC$ 2.60 to 2.70, to US$ 1.00. U.S. currency is freely accepted, but your change will be in EC dollars.

Most St. Kitts-Nevis islanders are descendants of African slaves imported by the British and French, the original American West Indian natives being long since extinct. The population is 94 percent black, 40 percent urban. English is the official and spoken language, but with a lilting West Indian accent, "mon."

The legal and judicial system, originally based on English common law, has now incorporated many of the basic elements of United States commercial law, especially that of New York and Delaware, for good reasons that will be clear in a moment.

The islands have a pleasant, healthy climate, warm with cool breezes throughout the year, low humidity and no real demarcated rainy season. Average annual rainfall is about 55 inches, most of it in the fall, which is also the hurricane season. The official tourist "season" is from December 15 to April 14, only because that's when weather is nastiest in the northern hemisphere and Caribbean islands most fashionable. Temperatures year-round average 78 to 85 degrees Fahrenheit, and from November through January the islands experience increased "Christmas winds," as they are called locally.

A low-key economic promotional program authorized by the 1984 "Citizenship Act" offers nationality and a passport in return for a $200,000 investment, usually the purchase price of a seaside condominium and certain "fees." Citizenship for the investor and spouse are included in the deal. (A less expensive route to citizenship is marriage, since St. Kitts & Nevis is one of the few countries that gives instant citizenship upon marriage to a spouse of either sex.)

Nevis is attractive for financial reasons, as we shall see, but it is also known for its natural beauty — long, curving beaches of white and black sand, lush foliage and flowers, mineral spa baths and restored sugar plantations now used as charming country inns, many nestled high in the mountains surrounded by lavish tropical gardens. For the energetic resident there is mountain climbing, swimming, tennis, horseback riding, snorkeling. But the going is easy here with hammocks for naps, lobster bakes on palm-shaded beaches, candlelight dinners in stately dining rooms and relaxation on romantic verandas.

Nevis is located two miles south of St. Kitts, a leisurely 45-minute ferry ride away, except Thursday, which is ship maintenance day, and the Sabbath. There is also inter-island air service.

The "Premier Off-Shore Corporate Jurisdiction"

That's the way local boosters describe the smaller of the two islands, Nevis, where its capital, Charlestown, has become a miniature international corporate business center.

About 1,200 of the island's 9,300 inhabitants live in the town, founded in 1660, a place full of ancient buildings with fanciful galleries, elaborate gingerbread woodwork, shutters, colorful hanging plants — and a small but effective cadre of international corporate and asset protection experts, both lawyers and bankers.

Based on the Island Assembly's adoption of the "Business Corporation Act of 1984," Nevis has an established, decade-long record of catering to foreign off shore corporations, with the welcome mat always out. Patterned after the extremely liberal (towards business) corporation laws of the American State of Delaware, English commercial law is also blended into the statute, so UK solicitors should have little fear about navigating its provisions.

The corporation statute allows complete confidentiality for company officials and shareholders, and there is no requirement for public disclosure of ownership, management, or financial status of a business.

Although they must pay an annual fee of US$450, "international business corporations," or "IBCs" as the law calls them, are otherwise exempt from taxes — no withholding, stamps, fees or taxes on income or foreign assets. Individually negotiated government-guaranteed tax holidays are available in writing for IBCs, provided they carry on no business locally. Official corporate start-up costs can be under US$1,000 including a minimum capitalization tax of US$200, and company formation fees of US$600. These low government levies compare very favorably with those imposed by other corporate-friendly havens, like the high-profile, high-cost Cayman Islands.

On Nevis there are no exchange controls, no tax treaties with other nations (including the U.S.), and the government will not exchange tax or other information with any other foreign revenue service or government. Principal corporate offices and records may be maintained by Nevis companies anywhere in the world the owners wish.

The Nevis corporation law is almost unique in that it contains a very modern legal provision allowing the international portability or transfer of an existing foreign company from its country of origin to the island. Known as the "redomiciling provision," this allows the smooth and instantaneous transfer of an existing American, British, Panamanian or any other nation's corporation, retention of its original name and date of incorporation — all without interruption of business activity or corporate existence. The only requirement is the amendment of existing articles of incorporation to conform with local laws.

New company creation and registration is fast in Nevis — accomplished by the simple payment of the capitalization tax and fees mentioned earlier to the Register of Corporations. Within ten days thereafter formal incorporation documents must be filed, but there are corporate service firms waiting to assist the foreign incorporator with ready-made paperwork.

Small wonder that in ten years since the law's original adoption, thousands of foreign corporate owners have established their companies in Charlestown, Nevis.

Asset Protection Trusts — A New Offshore Service

Building on their record for statutory corporate cordiality, on April 28, 1994 the Island Assembly adopted the "Nevis International Trust Ordinance," a comprehensive, clear and flexible asset protection trust (APT) law comparable to, and in many ways, better than that of the Cook Islands in the South Pacific, already well-known as an APT world center.

The new Nevis law incorporates the best features of the Cook Islands law, but in many ways is more flexible. The basic aim of the law is to permit foreign citizens to obtain protection against threats to their property and assets by transferring title to an APT established in Charlestown, Nevis.

Nevis simply is taking advantage of the fact that in many parts of the world, especially the U.S., medical, legal and professional malpractice law suits, as well as legislative and judicial imposition of no-fault personal liability on corporate officers and directors have become a nasty fact of business life. A Nevis trust places personal assets beyond the reach of potential foreign governments, litigious plaintiffs, creditors and contingent fee lawyers.

Under the new law, the Nevis judiciary will not recognize any non-domestic court orders regarding its domestic APTs. This forces a foreign judgment creditor to start all over again, retrying in Nevisian courts, with Nevisian lawyers, the original claim giving rise to the foreign judgment. A plaintiff who sues an APT must first post a US$25,000 bond with the government to cover court and others costs, before a suit will be accepted for filing. And the statute of limitations for filing legal challenges to a Nevisian APT runs out one year from the date of the trust creation. In cases where fraudulent intent on the part of the trust or its officers or beneficiaries is alleged, the law places the burden of proof on the foreign claimant.

Nevis has an established international bar and local trust experts who understand and can assist in furthering APT objectives. The APT act has proven very popular and a considerable number of trusts have been registered in Nevis.

Under the statute, basic trust documents are not required to be filed with the Nevis government, and are not a matter of public record. The only public information needed to establish an APT is a standard form or letter naming the trustee, the date of trust creation, the date of the filing, and the name of the local trust company representing the APT. The only governmental fee charged is US$200 upon filing, and an equal annual fee to maintain the filing.

Once established, the Nevis asset protection trust can consist of as little as a trust account in a local bank offering international services. Nevis has many of them, including Barclays International, Royal Bank of Canada, the Bank of Nova Scotia, the Bank of Commerce, the Nevis Co-operative Bank, the St.Kitts-Nevis-Anguilla Bank and the Nevis Bank in Charlestown. Banking hours vary but generally are 8-2 Monday through Thursday, Friday 8-5 and Saturday 8:30-11:00 a.m.

These established banks have full international departments. Most international banks offer U.S. dollar-denominated accounts that often pay better interest rates than U.S. institutions. With modern fax machines, telex, telephones, instant communications and international banking facilities, it is just as convenient to hold assets and accounts in Nevis as it is in any major financial center — and a lot safer in many personal and financial respects.

Under the provisions of the Nevis International Trust Ordinance, the same person can serve in the triple role of creator (settlor), beneficiary and protector of the APT, allowing far greater control over assets and income than U.S. domestic law permits. Generally, Anglo-American common law forbids a settlor to create a trust for his or her own benefit.

The basic structure of a foreign asset protection trust differs little from an Anglo-American trust.

The settlor creates the trust by executing a formal declaration describing the purposes, to which he transfers assets to be administered according to the declaration by the named trustees. Usually there are three trustees named, two in the settlor's country and one in Nevis, the latter known as a "protector." Named trust beneficiaries can vary according to the settlor's estate planning objectives, and under Nevis law the settlor may be the primary beneficiary.

Nevis requires the appointment of a trust "protector" who, as the title indicates, oversees its operation to insure trust objectives are met and the law is followed. A protector does not manage the trust, but possibly can veto some actions — and Nevis allows a beneficiary to serve in the dual role as protector.

Tax and Legal Advantages for American Readers

Under U.S. tax law, foreign asset protection trusts are "tax-neutral." They are considered as domestic trusts, meaning income from the trust is treated by the Internal Revenue Service as the settlor's personal income and taxed accordingly. Because the settlor retains some control over the transfer of his assets to any foreign trust, including those established in Nevis, U.S. gift taxes can usually be avoided. Although Nevis has no estate taxes, U.S. estate taxes are imposed on the value of trust assets for the settlor's estate, but all existing exemptions for combined martial assets can be used. Foreign asset protection trusts are not subject to the 35 percent U.S. excise tax otherwise imposed on transfers of property to a "foreign person."

One device a settlor may employ to retain optimal control of assets is to form a limited partnership, making the Nevisian trust a limited partner. This allows a general managing partner/settlor to retain active control over all assets he transfers to the Nevis trust/limited partner, while trust assets are protected from creditors or other legal assaults.

It goes without saying that assets located in the United States, title to which are held by a foreign APT, are certainly not immune from American court powers. U.S. judges have shown an increasing tendency to justify such jurisdiction, but in appropriate cases cash and certain types of portable personal property easily can be transferred physically to a foreign situs such as Nevis.

Nevis — An Obvious Choice

Aside from the undoubted protection offered by the new Nevis International Trust Ordinance, this is a small nation with great economic and political stability, a highly reputable judicial system, favorable local tax laws, no language barrier and excellent international communication and financial facilities.

These combined virtues of St. Kitts-Nevis explain why it is already taking its rightful place as a leader among other offshore financial centers with legal systems hospitable to foreign-owned asset protection trusts, among them the other Caribbean nations of the Cayman Islands, the Bahamas, Belize, the Turks and Caicos islands, the Cook Islands in the south Pacific near New Zealand, as well as Cyprus and Gibraltar in the Mediterranean.

The Nevis Business Corporation Ordinance 1984 - (as amended, 1999)

An Ordinance to provide for the establishment of business corporations in the island of Nevis and to provide for matters incidental or consequential thereto.

Be It Enacted by the Queen's Most Excellent Majesty by and with the advice and consent of the Nevis Island Assembly and by the Authority of the same as follows.

Part I - General Provisions

1. This Ordinance shall be known as the "**Nevis Business Corporation Ordinance 1984.**"

2. In this Ordinance, unless the context otherwise requires, the term:

"**Articles of incorporation**" includes

(i) the original articles of incorporation or any other instrument filed or issued under any law to form a domestic or foreign corporation, amended, supplemented, corrected or restated by articles of amendment, merger or consolidation, or other instruments filed or issued under any law; or

(ii) a special law or charter creating a domestic or foreign corporation, as amended, supplemented or restated.

"**Board**" means board of directors.

"**Corporation**" or "**domestic corporation**" means a corporation for profit formed under this Ordinance, or existing on its effective date and theretofore formed under any other ordinance of the Nevis Island Assembly.

"**Deputy Registrar**" means the person or persons appointed by the Minister to assist the Registrar of Companies in performing his duties under this Ordinance.

"**High Court**" means High Court having jurisdiction in St. Kitts and Nevis.

"**Insolvent**" means being unable to pay debts as they become due in the usual course of the debtor's business.

"**Minister of Finance**" means the Minister for the time being charged with the responsibility of Finance in the Nevis Island Administration.

"**Registrar of Companies**" means the person appointed by the Minister to perform the duties of Registrar under this Ordinance.

"**Treasury shares**" means shares which have been issued, have been subsequently acquired, and are retained uncancelled by the corporation.

3.(1) Any corporation or company created prior to the effective date of this Ordinance may at any time subject itself to the provisions of this Ordinance by amending its articles of incorporation in accordance with the manner prescribed by Part IX. Any corporation formed or subject to this Ordinance which does business in Nevis shall be subject to and comply with all requirements of the Companies Act (Chapter 335) in the same manner as a company formed thereunder.

(2) A corporation to which the Banking Law or Insurance Law is applicable shall also be subject to this Ordinance, but the Banking Law or Insurance Law, as the case may be, shall prevail over any conflicting provisions of this Ordinance.

4.(1) Whenever any provision of this Ordinance requires any instrument to be filed with the Registrar of Companies, such instrument shall comply with the provisions of this Part unless otherwise expressly provided by a law.

(2) Every instrument referenced herein, filed or required to be filed, shall be in the English language, except that the corporate name may be in another language if written in English letters or characters.

(3) All instruments shall be signed by all directors; or, by the president, vice president or managing director, and by the secretary or an assistant secretary.

(4) Whenever any provision of this Ordinance requires an instrument to be acknowledged, such requirement means in the case of execution of an instrument within Nevis that:

> *(i)* The person signing the instrument shall acknowledge that it is his act and deed or that it is the act and deed of the corporation, as the case may be; and

> *(ii)* The instrument shall be acknowledged before a notary public, commissioner for oaths or other person authorized to take acknowledgments, who shall attest that he knows the person making the acknowledgment to be the person who executed the instrument.

(5) In the case of the execution of an instrument outside of Nevis, an acknowledgment shall mean:

> *(i)* The person signing the instrument shall acknowledge that it is his act and deed or that it is the act and deed of the corporation, as the case may be; and

> *(ii)* The instrument shall be acknowledged before a notary public or any other person authorized to take acknowledgments according to the laws of the place of execution, or a consul or vice-consul of St. Kitts and Nevis or other governmental official of St. Kitts or Nevis authorized to take acknowledgments or, in their absence. a consular official of another government having diplomatic relations with

St. Kitts and Nevis, and such notary, person, consul or vice-consul shall attest that he knows the person making the acknowledgment to be the person who executed the instrument; and

(iii) When the acknowledgment shall be taken by a notary public or any other person authorized to take acknowledgments, except a governmental official of St. Kitts or Nevis or foreign consular official, the signature of such person who has authority shall be attested to by a consul or vice-consul of the Nation of St. Kitts and Nevis or, in his absence, by a consular official of another government having diplomatic relations with St. Kitts and Nevis, or a government official of the place of execution who is authorized to make such attestation, or an Apostille according to the Convention de la Haye de 5 Octobre 1961.

(6) Whenever any provision of this Ordinance requires any instrument to be filed with the Registrar of Companies, such requirement means that:

(i) An appropriate receipt evidencing payment of all appropriate fees shall be delivered to the office of the Registrar of Companies and, within ten days of the date of the receipt, the original instrument together with a duplicate instrument, both signed and acknowledged;

(ii) Upon delivery of the original signed and acknowledged instrument with the required receipt and an exact signed and acknowledged copy, the Registrar of Companies shall certify that the instrument has been filed in his office by endorsing the

word "Filed" and the date of the required receipt upon the original instrument. Said date shall be the filing date;

(iii) The Registrar of Companies shall compare the duplicate signed and acknowledged copy with the original signed and acknowledged instrument, and if he finds that the text is identical, shall affix on the duplicate copy the same endorsement of filing as he affixed on the original. The said original, as endorsed, shall be returned to the corporation. The endorsement constitutes the certificate of the Registrar of Companies that the document is a true copy of the instrument filed in his office and that it was filed as of the date stated in the endorsement; and

(iv) Any instrument filed in accordance with subsection (ii) shall be effective as of the filing date stated thereon.

(7) Any instrument relating to a domestic or foreign Corporation and filed with the Registrar of Companies under this Ordinance may be corrected with respect to any error apparent on the face or defect in the execution thereof by filing with the Registrar of Companies a certificate of correction, executed and acknowledged in the manner required for the original instrument. The certificate of correction shall specify the error or defect to be corrected and shall set forth the portion of the instrument in correct form. The corrected instrument when filed shall be effective as of the date the original instrument was filed.

5. All certificates issued by the Registrar of Companies in accordance with the provisions of this Ordinance and all copies of documents filed in his office in accordance with the provisions of this Ordinance shall, when certified by him, be taken and received in all courts, public offices and official bodies as prima facie evidence of the facts therein stated and of the execution of such instruments.

6.(1) The Minister of Finance is hereby empowered to promulgate and shall so promulgate a schedule of fees for the filing and issuance of documents under this Ordinance. Fees payable in respect of this Ordinance shall be payable in Eastern Caribbean dollars, or, upon the authorization of the Minister of Finance, in a currency other than that of the Nation of St. Kitts and Nevis.

(2) On filing with the Registrar of Companies an amendment of articles of incorporation increasing the authorized number of shares or articles of merger or consolidation of two or more domestic corporations, a fee shall be paid computed in accordance with the schedule promulgated pursuant to section (I) on the basis of the number of shares provided for in the articles of amendment or articles of merger or consolidation, except that all fees paid by the corporation with respect to the shares authorized prior to such amendment or merger or consolidation shall be deducted from the amount to be paid.

(3) On filing with the Registrar of Companies an amendment of articles of incorporation other than an amendment increasing the authorized number of shares, or articles of dissolution, or articles of merger or consolidation into a foreign corporation or any other document for which a certificate is issued under this Ordinance, a fee shall be paid in accordance with the schedule promulgated pursuant to section (1).

(4) Fees for certifying copies of documents and for filing, recording or indexing papers shall be fixed by the Minister of Finance.

7. Every corporation shall pay to the Minister of Finance an annual fee as prescribed in the schedule required to be promulgated by the Minister of Finance under this Ordinance.

8. Whenever any notice is required to be given to any shareholder or director or bondholder of a corporation or to any other person under the provisions of this Ordinance or under the provisions of the articles of incorporation or bylaws of the corporation, a waiver thereof in writing, signed by the person or persons entitled to such notice, whether before or after the time stated therein, shall be deemed to be equivalent to the giving of such notice.

9. Any notice or information required to be given to shareholders of bearer shares shall be provided in the manner designated in the corporation's articles of incorporation or bylaws or, if the notice can no longer be provided as stated therein, the notice shall be published in a publication of general circulation in Nevis or in a place where the corporation has a place of business. Any notice requiring a shareholder to take action in order to secure a right or privilege shall be published or given in time to allow a reasonable opportunity for such action to be taken.

10. In construing this Ordinance, or any part hereof, the Courts or any other person shall refer to the common law or to the construction of the same or similar acts in other jurisdictions.

Part II - Corporate Purposes And Powers

11. Corporations may be organized under this Ordinance for any lawful business purpose or purposes.

12. Subject to any limitations provided in this Ordinance or any other law of Nevis or its articles of incorporation, every corporation shall have power in furtherance of its corporate purposes irrespective of corporate benefit and whether or not enumerated in its articles:

(1) To have perpetual succession.

(2) To sue and be sued in all courts of competent jurisdiction.

(3) To have a corporate seal, and to alter such seal at pleasure, and to use it by causing it or a facsimile to be affixed or impressed or reproduced in any other manner.

(4) To purchase, receive, take by grant, gift, devise, bequest, or otherwise, lease or otherwise acquire, own, hold, improve, employ, use and otherwise deal in and with, real or personal property, or any interest therein, wherever situated.

(5) To sell, convey, lease, exchange, transfer or otherwise dispose of, or mortgage or pledge, or create a security interest in, all or any of its real or personal property, or any interest therein.

(6) To purchase, take, receive, subscribe for, or otherwise acquire, own, hold, vote, employ, sell, lend, lease, exchange, transfer, or otherwise dispose of, mortgage, and pledge, bonds and other obligations, shares, or other securities or interests issued by others, whether engaged in similar or different business, governmental, or other activities.

(7) To make contracts, give guarantees and incur liabilities, borrow money at such rates of interest as the corporation may determine, issue its notes, bonds, and other obligations, and secure any of its obligations by mortgage or pledge of all or any of its property or any interest therein, wherever situated, in any currency.

(8) To lend money, invest and reinvest its funds, and take and hold real and personal property as security for the payment of funds so loaned or invested, in any currency.

(9) To do business, carry on its operations, and have offices and exercise the powers granted by this Part in any jurisdiction within or without Nevis.

(10) To elect or appoint officers, managing directors, employees and other agents of the corporation, define their duties, fix their compensation, and the compensation of directors, and to indemnify corporate personnel.

(11) To adopt, amend or repeal bylaws relating to the business of the corporation, the conduct of its affairs, its rights or powers or the rights or powers of its shareholders, directors or officers.

(12) To make donations for the public welfare or for charitable, educational, scientific, civic or similar purposes.

(13) To pay pensions and establish pension plans, pension trusts, profit sharing plans, stock bonus plans, stock option plans and other incentive plans for any or all of its directors, officers, and employees.

(14) To purchase, receive, take, or otherwise acquire, own, hold, sell, lend, exchange, transfer or otherwise dispose of, pledge, use and otherwise deal in and with its own shares.

(15) To be a promoter, incorporator, partner, member, associate, or manager of any partnership, corporation, joint venture, trust or other enterprise.

(16) To have and exercise all powers necessary or convenient to effect any or all of the purposes for which the corporation is formed.

(17) To be recognized and to be domiciled or domesticated within or without Nevis, and to change the situs of said domicile or domestication from time to time.

(18) To protect the assets of the corporation for the benefit of the corporation, its creditors and its members, and at the discretion of the directors, for any person having a direct or in direct interest in the company.

13. A guarantee may be given by a corporation not in furtherance of its corporate purposes, when authorized at a meeting of shareholders by vote of the holders of a majority of all outstanding shares entitled to vote thereon. If authorized by a like vote, such guarantee may be secured by a mortgage or pledge of, or the creation of a security interest in, all or any part of the corporate property, or any interest therein, wherever situated.

14. No act of a corporation and no transfer of real or personal property to or by a corporation, otherwise lawful, shall be invalid by reason of the fact that the corporation was without capacity or power to do such act or to make or receive such transfer, but such lack of capacity or power may be asserted:

(i) In an action by a shareholder against the corporation to enjoin the doing of any act or the transfer of real or personal property by or to the corporation. If the unauthorized act or transfer sought to be enjoined is being, or is to be, performed or made under any contract to which the corporation is a party, the court may, if all of the parties to the contract are parties to the action and if it deems the same to be equitable, set aside and enjoin the performance of such contract, and in so doing may allow to the corporation or to the other parties to the contract, as the case may be, such compensation as may be equitable for the loss or damage sustained by any of them from the action of the court in setting aside and enjoining the performance of such contract; provided that anticipated profits to be derived from the performance of the contract shall not be awarded by the court as a loss or damage sustained;

(ii) In an action by the corporation, whether acting directly or through a receiver, trustee, or other legal representative, or through shareholders in a derivative suit against the incumbent or former officers or directors of the corporation for loss or damage due to their unauthorized act; and

(iii) In a proceeding by the High Court to dissolve the corporation, or to enjoin it from the doing of unauthorized business.

15. A corporation shall be a legal entity considered in law a fictional person with separate rights and liabilities, distinct from its shareholders or members. The corporation shall be a proper plaintiff in a suit to assert a legal right of the corporation and a proper defendant in a suit to assert a legal right against the corporation; and the naming of a shareholder, member, director, officer or employee of the corporation as a party to a suit in Nevis or elsewhere to represent the corporation is subject to a motion to dismiss if such party is the sole party to sue or defend, or subject to a motion for misjoinder if such party is joined with another party who is a proper party and has been joined only to represent the corporation.

16. Unless otherwise provided by law, the directors, officers, employees and shareholders of a corporation shall not be liable for corporate debts and obligations.

Part III - Service Of Process; Registered Agent

17.(1) A corporation subject to this Ordinance shall at all times have a registered agent in St. Christopher and Nevis . A corporation which fails to maintain a registered agent in St. Christopher and Nevis shall be in contravention of this Ordinance.

(2) Service of process on a registered agent may be made by registered mail addressed to the registered agent or in any other manner provided by law for the service of summons as if the registered agent were a defendant.

(3) Any registered agent of a corporation may resign as such agent upon filing a written notice thereof, executed in duplicate, with the Registrar of Companies, who shall cause a copy thereof to be sent by registered mail to the corporation at the address of the office of the corporation or, if none, at the last known address of a person at whose request the corporation was formed. No designation of a new registered agent shall be accepted for filing unless all charges owing to the former agent shall have been paid.

(4) A designation of a registered agent under this section may be made, revoked, or changed by filing an appropriate notification with the Registrar of Companies.

(5) The designation of a registered agent shall terminate upon the expiration of thirty days written notice of resignation directed to the corporation and the filing of a copy of said notice of resignation with the Registrar of Companies; or sooner if a successor agent is designated.

(6) A registered agent, when served with process, notice or demand for the corporation which he represents, shall transmit the same to the corporation by personal notification or in the following manner: Upon receipt of the process, notice or demand, the registered agent shall cause a copy of such paper to be mailed to the corporation named therein at its last known address. Such mailing shall be by registered mail. As soon thereafter as possible if process was issued in Nevis, the registered agent may file with the clerk of the court issuing the process either the receipt of such registered mailing or an affidavit stating that such mailing has been made, signed by the registered agent, or if the agent is a corporation, by an officer of the same, properly notarized. Compliance with the provisions of this section shall relieve the registered agent from any further obligation to the corporation for service of the process, notice or demand, but the agent's failure to comply with the provisions of this section shall in no way affect the validity of the service of the process, notice or demand.

(7) Only a barrister of solicitor admitted to practice in St. Christopher and Nevis or a corporation having a paid-in capital of at least $500,000.00 may act as registered agent.

(8) No barrister or solicitor or corporation shall act as registered agent unless first licensed by the Minister. The original application for licensing shall be in the prescribed form and accompanied by the prescribed fee and there shall be an annual fee payable in January of each year.

(9) The Minister shall prescribe fees for the licensing of registered agents under this Ordinance.

18.(1) Whenever a corporation subject to this Ordinance fails to maintain an authorized agent in Nevis, or whenever said registered agent cannot with reasonable diligence be found at his business address, then the Registrar of Companies or his appointee shall be an agent of such corporation upon whom any process or notice or demand required or permitted by law to be served may be served.

(2) Service on the Registrar of Companies or his appointee as agent of a corporation shall be made by personally delivering to and leaving with him or his deputy or with any person authorized by the Registrar of Companies to receive such service, at the office of the Registrar of Companies, duplicate copies of such process together with the statutory fee. The Registrar of Companies or his appointee shall promptly send one of such copies by registered mail, return receipt requested, to such corporation at the business address of its registered agent, or if there is no such office, then the Registrar of Companies or his appointee shall mail such copy in care of any director named in the articles of incorporation at his address stated therein or at the address of the corporation without Nevis, or if none, at the last known address of a person at whose request the corporation was formed or in any other manner permitted by Law.

19. The Registrar of Companies shall keep a record of each process served upon the Registrar of Companies or his appointee under this Part, including the date of service. It shall, upon request made within five years of such service, issue a certificate under its seal certifying as to the receipt of the process by an authorized person, the date and place of such service, and the receipt of the statutory fee.

20. Nothing contained in this Part shall affect the validity of service of process on a corporation effected in any other manner permitted by law.

Part IV - Formation Of Corporations; Corporate Names

21. Any person, partnership, association or corporation, singly or jointly with others, and without regard to his or their residence, domicile, or jurisdiction of incorporation, may incorporate or organize a corporation under this Ordinance.

22.(1) Except as otherwise provided in subsection (2) of this section, the name of a corporation:

> *(i)* Shall contain the word "corporation", "incorporated", "company", or "limited" or other words or an abbreviation of one of such or other words as will clearly indicate that it is a corporation as distinguished from a natural person or partnership; and

> *(ii)* Shall not be the same as the name of a corporation of any type or kind, as such name appears on the index of names of existing corporations or companies or on the reserved name list maintained by the Registrar of Companies or a name so similar to any such name as to tend to confuse or deceive.

(2) The provisions of subsection (1) of this section shall not:

> *(i)* Require any corporation, existing or authorized to do business on the effective date of this ordinance, to add to, modify or otherwise change its corporate name; and

> *(ii)* Prevent a corporation with which another corporation, domestic or foreign, is merged, or which is formed by the reorganization or consolidation of one or more domestic or foreign corporations, or upon a sale, lease or other disposition

17

to or exchange with, a domestic corporation of all or substantially all the assets of another domestic corporation, including its name, from having the same name as any of such corporations if at the time such other corporation was existing under the laws of Nevis or was authorized to do business in Nevis.

23. The Registrar of Companies shall keep an alphabetical index of all reserved names and those of all corporations subject to this Ordinance together with those other names required to be kept by the Registrar of Companies by law.

24.(1) Any person, natural or corporate, or any agent thereof may reserve a name with the Registrar of Companies provided said reservation is made in accordance with this Part and is made in good faith for subsequent use in formation of a corporation under this Ordinance or for use in changing the name of a corporation already subject to this Ordinance. A name may be reserved under Parts XII or XIII by a non-Nevisian corporation which has filed for a transfer of domicile thereunder. Such name reservation shall not be subject to the time limitation and fee requirements of section 24.(4) of this chapter.

(**2**) An application to reserve a name shall be delivered to the Registrar of Companies together with the required fee. Said application shall set forth:

(i) the name to be reserved;

(ii) the name and address of the applicant;

(iii) a statement of the reasons for the application in accordance with section (l) above; and

      (iv) the name in which the Certificate of Name Reservation is to be issued.

(3)   Provided the name to be reserved is available for use, the Registrar of Companies shall enter the name upon the reserved name list and issue a Certificate of Name Reservation in the name of the applicant or in the name designated by the applicant. The Certificate of Name Reservation shall set forth:

      (i) the information contained in the application therefor; and

      (ii) the date the name was entered upon the reserved name list; which date shall be the date of reservation.

(4)   Beginning upon the date of reservation, the name reserved will be maintained upon the reserved name list by the Registrar of Companies and shall not be used except by the person, natural or corporate, in whose name the Certificate of Name Reservation has been issued. Said reservation shall terminate upon the expiration of one hundred twenty days next following the date of reservation unless sooner renewed. Upon payment of the required fees, the reservation shall be renewed with the Registrar of Companies for no more than two like periods. An appropriate receipt for the required fees shall be taken along with the Certificate of Name Reservation to be proof of the extension of the reservation.

(5) The Certificate of Name Reservation and any renewals thereof shall be evidenced to the Registrar of Companies at the time the name reserved is utilized by the person, natural or corporate, in whose name said Certificate of Name Reservation has been issued.

25. The articles of incorporation shall set forth:

(1) The name of the corporation;

(2) A statement that the corporation is formed under this Ordinance;

(3) The succession of the corporation if other than perpetual;

(4) The purpose or purposes for which the corporation is organized. It shall be sufficient to state, either alone or with other businesses or purposes, that the purpose of the corporation is to engage in any lawful act or activity for which corporations may be organized under this Ordinance, and by such statement all lawful acts and activities shall be within the purposes of the corporation, except for express limitations, if any.

(5) The address of the corporation in Nevis which shall be the address of its registered agent.

(6) The aggregate number of shares which the corporation shall have authority to issue; if such shares are to consist of one class only, the par value of each of such shares, or a statement that all of such shares are without par value; or if such shares are to be divided into classes, the number of shares of each class, and a statement of the par value of the shares of each class or that such shares are to be without par value.

(7) If the shares are to be divided into classes, the designation of each class and a statement of the preferences, limitations, and relative rights in respect of the shares of each class.

(8) The number of shares to be issued as registered shares and as bearer shares and whether registered shares may be exchanged for bearer shares and bearer shares for registered shares.

(9) If bearer shares are authorized to be issued,

(i) appropriate procedural provisions respecting the rights and obligations of bearer shareholders including those relating to

(1) notice of meetings or other action,

(2) payment of dividends and,

(3) qualification for voting; or,

(ii) a statement that the provisions required by (i) above shall be set forth in the bylaws.

(10) If the corporation is to issue the shares of any preferred or special class in series, then the designation of each series and a statement of the variations in the relative rights and preferences as between series insofar as the same are to be fixed in the articles of incorporation, and a statement of any authority to be vested in the board of directors to establish series and fix and determine the variations in the relative rights and preferences as between series.

(11) If the initial directors are to be named in the articles of incorporation, the names and addresses of the persons who are to serve as directors until the first annual meeting of the shareholders or until their successors shall be elected and qualify.

(12) The name and address of each incorporator.

(13) Any provision, not inconsistent with law, which the incorporators elect to set forth in the articles of incorporation for the regulation of the affairs of the corporation, including the designation of initial directors, subscription of stock by the

incorporators, and any provision restricting the transfer of shares or providing for greater quorum or voting requirements with respect to shareholders or directors than are otherwise prescribed in this Ordinance, and any provision which under this Ordinance is required or permitted to be set forth in the bylaws.

It shall not be necessary to enumerate in the articles of incorporation the general corporate powers stated in section 12 of Part II

26. The articles of incorporation may confer upon the holders of any bonds, debentures, or other obligations issued rights of or to be issued by the corporation, whether secured by mortgage or otherwise or unsecured, any one or more of the following powers and rights:

Any other rights to information concerning the financial condition of the corporation which its shareholders have or may have.

27. Articles of incorporation shall be signed and acknowledged by each incorporator and filed with the Registrar of Companies in conformity with the provisions of Part I of this Ordinance.

28. The corporate existence shall, upon filing the articles of incorporation, be effective as of the filing date stated thereon. The endorsebment by the Registrar of Companies, as required by section 4 of Part I, shall be conclusive evidence that all conditions precedent required to be performed by the incorporators have been complied with and that the corporation has been incorporated under this Ordinance.

29.(1) Within a reasonable time after the filing of the articles of incorporation, an organization meeting shall be held either within or without Nevis. The said organization meeting shall be held, in person or by proxy, by the initial directors named in the articles of incorporation or by the incorporator or incorporators or their transferees pursuant to subsection (2) hereof. The purpose of the meeting shall be to adopt bylaws, transact such business as may come before the meeting, do such acts to perfect the organization of the corporation as are deemed appropriate and, if the initial directors are not named in the articles of incorporation, elect directors to serve or hold office until the first annual meeting of shareholders or until their successors are elected and qualify.

(2) If the articles of incorporation state that the incorporators have subscribed for stock, such subscriptions may be transferred prior to the organization meeting of directors and such transferees may hold the organization meeting of incorporators.

(3) Any action permitted to be taken at the organization meeting may be taken without a meeting if each incorporator, transferee or director signs an instrument setting forth the action so taken.

30. (1) Every corporation formed under this Ordinance shall have bylaws.

(2) The initial bylaws of a corporation may be adopted by its board of directors. Except as otherwise provided in the articles of incorporation, bylaws may be amended, repealed or adopted by vote of the shareholders. If so provided in the articles of incorporation or a bylaw adopted by the shareholders, bylaws may also be amended, repealed or adopted by the board of directors, but any bylaw adopted by the directors may be amended or repealed by shareholders entitled to vote thereon.

(3) The bylaws shall contain appropriate procedural provisions respecting the rights and obligations of bearer shareholders as set forth in section 25 of this Part IV in the event the articles of incorporation do not contain such provisions.

(4) The bylaws may contain any provision relating to the business of the corporation, the conduct of its affairs, its rights or powers or the rights or powers of its shareholders, directors or officers, not inconsistent with this Ordinance or any other Law of Nevis or the articles of incorporation.

Part V - Corporate Finance

31.(1) Every corporation shall have power to issue the number of shares stated in its articles of incorporation. Such shares may be of one or more classes or one or more series within any class thereof, any or all of which classes may be of shares with par value or shares without par value, and may be registered or bearer shares, with such voting powers, full or limited, or without voting powers and in such series and with such designations, preferences and relative, participating, optional or special rights and qualifications, limitations or restrictions thereon as shall be stated in the articles of incorporation or in the resolution providing for the issue of such shares adopted by the board of directors pursuant to authority expressly vested in it by the provisions of the articles of incorporation.

(2) The articles of incorporation or the resolution providing for the issue of shares adopted by the board of directors may provide that shares of any class of shares or of any series of shares within any class thereof shall be convertible into the shares of one or more other classes of shares or series except into shares of a class or series having rights or preferences as to dividends or distribution of assets upon liquidation which are prior or superior in rank to those of the shares being converted.

(3) A corporation may provide in its articles of incorporation for one or more classes or series of shares which are redeemable, in whole or in part, at the option of the corporation at such price or prices, within such period and under such conditions as are stated in the articles of incorporation or in the resolution providing for the issue of such shares adopted by the board of directors pursuant to authority expressly vested in it by the provisions of the articles of incorporation.

(4) A corporation may issue fractional shares.

(5) Before any corporation shall issue any shares of any class or of any series of any class of which the voting powers, designations, preferences and relative, participating, optional or other rights, if any, or the qualifications, limitations, or restrictions thereof, if any, have not been set forth in the articles of incorporation, but are provided for in a resolution adopted by the board of directors pursuant to authority expressly vested in it by the provisions of the articles of incorporation, a statement setting forth a copy of such resolution and the number of shares of the class or series to be issued shall be executed, acknowledged, and filed in accordance with section 4 of Part I of this Ordinance. Upon the filing of such statement, the resolution establishing and designating the class or series and fixing the relative rights and preferences thereof shall become effective and shall constitute an amendment of the articles of incorporation.

32.(1) A restriction on the transfer of shares of a corporation may be imposed either by the articles of incorporation or by the bylaws or by an agreement among any number of shareholders or among such shareholders and the corporation. No restriction so imposed shall be binding with respect to shares issued prior to the adoption of the restriction unless the holders of such shares are parties to an agreement or voted in favor of the restriction. Any restriction which absolutely prohibits the transfer of shares shall be null and void.

(2) Restrictions on the transfer of shares include those which:

> *(i)* Obligate the holder of the restricted shares to offer to the corporation or to any other holders of securities of the corporation or to any person or to any combination of the foregoing, a prior opportunity, to be exercised within a reasonable time, to acquire the restricted shares; or

(ii) Obligate the corporation or any holder of shares of the corporation or any other person or any combination of the foregoing, to purchase at a specified price the shares which are the subject of an agreement respecting the purchase and sale of the restricted securities.

(3) Any transfer restriction adopted under this section shall be noted on the face or the back of the stock certificate.

(4) Any person becoming entitled by operation of law or otherwise to a share or shares in consequence of the death, insanity or bankruptcy of any shareholder of a corporation incorporated under this Ordinance may be registered as a shareholder upon such evidence being produced as may reasonably be required by the directors. An application by any such person to be registered as a shareholder shall for all purposes be deemed a transfer of shares of the deceased, insane or bankrupt shareholder and the directors shall treat it as such.

33.(1) A subscription for shares of a corporation to be organized shall be irrevocable for a period of six months from its date unless otherwise provided by the terms of the subscription agreement or unless all of the subscribers consent to the revocation of such subscription.

(2) A subscription, whether made before or after the formation of a corporation, shall not be enforceable unless in writing and signed by the subscriber.

(3) Unless otherwise provided in the subscription agreement, subscriptions for shares, whether made before or after the organization of a corporation, shall be paid in full at such time, or in such installments and at such times, as shall be determined by the board of directors. Any call made by the board of directors for payment on subscriptions shall be uniform as to all shares of the class or as to all shares of the same series, as the case may be.

(4) In case of default in the payment of any installment or call when such payment is due, the corporation may proceed to collect the amount due in the same manner as any debt due the corporation. The bylaws may prescribe a penalty for failure to pay installments or calls that may become due, but no penalty working a forfeiture of a subscription, or of the amounts paid thereon, shall be declared as against any subscriber unless the amount due thereon shall remain unpaid for a period of thirty days after written demand has been made therefor. If mailed, such written demand shall be deemed to be made when sent by registered mail addressed to the subscriber at his last post office address known to the corporation. In the event of the sale of any shares by reason of any forfeiture, the excess of proceeds realized over the amount due and unpaid on such shares shall be paid to the delinquent subscriber or to his legal representative. If no prospective purchaser offers a cash price sufficient to pay the full balance owed by the delinquent subscriber plus the expenses incidental to such sale, the shares subscribed for shall be cancelled and restored to the status of authorized but unissued shares and all previous payments thereon shall be forfeited to the corporation and transferred to surplus.

(5) Subscriptions for shares of stock are transferable unless otherwise provided in a subscription agreement.

34.(1) Consideration for the issue of shares shall consist of money or other property, tangible or intangible, or labor or for shares-services actually received by or performed for the corporation or for its benefit or in its formation or reorganization, or a combination thereof. In the absence of fraud in the transaction, the judgment of the board of directors or shareholders, as the case may be, as to the value of the consideration received for shares shall be conclusive.

(2) Shares with par value may be issued for such consideration, not less than the par value thereof, as is fixed from time to time by the board

(3) Shares without par value may be issued for such consideration as is fixed from time to time by the board unless the articles of incorporation reserve to the shareholders the right to fix the consideration. If such right is reserved as to any shares, a vote of the shareholders shall either fix the consideration to be received for the shares or authorize the board to fix such consideration.

(4) Treasury shares may be disposed of by a corporation on such terms and conditions as are fixed from time to time by the board.

(5) That part of the surplus of a corporation which is transferred to stated capital upon the issuance of shares as a share dividend shall be deemed to be the consideration for the issuance of such shares.

35.(1) Neither obligations of the subscriber for future payments nor future service shall constitute payment or part payment for shares of a corporation.

(2) Certificates for shares may not be issued until the full amount of consideration therefor has been paid.

(3) When the consideration for shares has been paid in full, the subscriber shall be entitled to all rights and privileges of a holder of such shares and to a certificate representing his shares, and such shares shall be deemed fully paid and nonassessable.

36. The reasonable charges and expenses of formation or reorganization of a corporation, and the reasonable expenses of and compensation for the sale or underwriting of its shares may be paid or allowed by the corporation out of the consideration received by it in payment for its shares without thereby rendering such shares not fully paid or assessable.

37.(1) Upon issue by a corporation of shares with a par value not in excess of the authorized shares, the consideration received therefor shall constitute stated capital to the extent of the par value of such shares, and the excess, if any, of such consideration shall constitute surplus.

(2) Upon issue by a corporation of shares without par value not in excess of the authorized shares, the entire consideration received therefor shall constitute stated capital unless the board within a period of sixty days after issue allocates to surplus a portion, but not all, of the consideration received for such shares. No such allocation shall be made of any portion of the consideration received for shares without par value having a preference in the assets of the corporation upon involuntary liquidation except all or part of the amount, if any, of such consideration in excess of such preference, nor shall such allocation be made of any portion of the consideration for the issue of shares without par value which is fixed by the shareholders pursuant to a right reserved in the articles of incorporation unless such allocation is authorized by vote of the shareholders.

(3) The stated capital of a corporation may be increased from time to time by resolution of the board of directors transferring all or part of surplus of the corporation to stated capital.

38.(1) The shares of a corporation shall be represented by certificates signed by the president, vice president, or managing director and the secretary or an assistant secretary or the treasurer or an assistant treasurer or director of the corporation, and may be sealed with the seal of the corporation, if any, or a facsimile thereof. The signatures of the officers upon a certificate may be facsimilies if the certificate is countersigned by a transfer agent or registered by a registrar other than the corporation itself or its employees. In case any officer who has signed or whose facsimile signature has been placed upon a certificate shall have ceased to be such officer before such certificate is issued, it may be issued by the corporation with the same effect as if he were such officer at the date of issue.

(2) Shares may be issued either in registered form or in bearer form provided that the articles of incorporation or bylaws prescribe the manner in which any required notice is to be given to shareholders of bearer shares in conformity with section 25 of Part IV. The transfer of bearer shares shall be by delivery of the certificates. The articles of incorporation may provide that on request of a shareholder his bearer shares shall be exchanged for registered shares or his registered shares exchanged for bearer shares.

(3) Each certificate representing shares issued by a corporation which is authorized to issue shares of more than one class shall set forth upon the face or back of the certificate, or shall state that the corporation will furnish to any shareholder upon request and without charge, a full statement of the designation, relative rights, preferences and limitations of the shares of each class authorized to be issued and, if the corporation is authorized to issue any class of preferred shares in series, the designation, relative rights, preferences and limitations of each such series so far as the same have been fixed and the authority of the board to designate and fix the relative rights, preferences and limitations of other series.

(4) Each certificate representing shares shall when issued state upon the face thereof:

> *(i)* That the corporation is formed under the laws of Nevis;

(ii) The name of the person or persons to whom issued if a registered share;

(iii) The number and class of shares, and the designation of the series, if any, which such certificate represents;

(iv) The par value of each share represented by such certificate, or a statement that the shares are without par value; and

(v) If the share does not entitle the holder to vote, that it is nonvoting, or if the right to vote exists only under certain circumstances, that the right to vote is limited.

39.(1) A corporation may declare and pay dividends in cash, stock or other property on its outstanding shares, except when currently the corporation is insolvent or would thereby be made insolvent or when the declaration or payment would be contrary to any restrictions contained in the articles of incorporation. Dividends may be declared and paid out of surplus only; but in case there is no surplus, dividends may be declared or paid out of the net profits for the fiscal year in which the dividend is declared and for the preceding fiscal year.

(2) A corporation engaged in the exploitation of natural resources or other wasting assets, including patents, or formed primarily for the liquidation of specific assets, may declare and pay dividends regardless of any surplus from the net profits derived from the liquidation or exploitation of such assets without making any deduction for the depletion of such assets resulting from lapse of time, consumption, liquidation or exploitation of such assets if the net assets remaining after such dividends are sufficient to cover the liquidation preferences of shares having such preferences in involuntary liquidation.

40.(1) A corporation may make pro rata distribution of its authorized but unissued shares to holders of any class or series of its outstanding shares subject to the following conditions:

> *(i)* If a distribution of shares having a par value is made, such shares shall be issued at not less than the par value thereof and there shall be transferred to stated capital at the time of such distribution an amount of surplus equal to the aggregate par value of such shares; and

> *(ii)* If a distribution of shares without par value is made, the amount of stated capital to be represented by each such share shall be fixed by the board, unless the articles of incorporation reserved to the shareholders the right to fix the consideration for the issue of such shares; and there shall be transferred to stated capital at the time of such distribution an amount of surplus equal to the aggregate stated capital represented by such shares.

(2) Unrealized appreciation of assets, if any, shall not be included in the computation of surplus available for a share dividend.

(3) Upon the payment of a dividend payable in shares, notice shall be given to the shareholders of the amount per share transferred from surplus.

(4) No dividend payable in shares of any class shall be paid unless the share dividend is specifically authorized by the vote of two-thirds of the shares of each class that might be adversely affected by such a share dividend.

(5) A split-up or division of the issued shares of any class into a greater number of shares of the same class without increasing the stated capital of the corporation shall not be construed to be a share dividend within the meaning of this section.

41.(1) A corporation, subject to any restrictions contained in its articles of incorporation, may purchase its own shares or redeem its redeemable shares out of surplus except when currently the corporation is insolvent or would thereby be made insolvent.

(2) A corporation may purchase its own shares out of stated capital except when currently the corporation is insolvent or would thereby be made insolvent, if the purchase is made for the purpose of:

(i) Eliminating fractions of shares;

(ii) Collecting or compromising indebtedness to the corporation; or

(iii) Paying dissenting shareholders entitled to receive payment for their shares under Parts IX or X.

(3) A corporation, subject to any restrictions contained in its articles of incorporation, may redeem or purchase its redeemable shares out of stated capital except when currently the corporation is insolvent or would thereby be made insolvent and except when such redemption or purchase would reduce net assets below the stated capital remaining after giving effect to the cancellation of such redeemable shares.

(4) When its redeemable shares are purchased by a corporation within the period of redeemability, the purchase price thereof shall not exceed the applicable redemption price stated in the articles of incorporation. Upon a call for redemption, the amount payable by the corporation for shares having a cumulative preference on dividends may include the stated redemption price plus accrued dividends to the next dividend date following the date of redemption of such shares.

42.(1) Shares that have been issued and have been purchased, redeemed or otherwise reacquired by a corporation shall be cancelled if they are reacquired out of stated capital, or if they are converted shares, or if the articles of incorporation require that such shares be cancelled upon reacquisition.

(2) Any shares reacquired by the corporation and not required to be cancelled may be either retained as treasury shares or cancelled by the board at the time of reacquisition or at any time thereafter.

(3) Neither the retention of reacquired shares as treasury shares, nor their subsequent distribution to shareholders or disposition for a consideration shall change the stated capital. Treasury shares may be disposed of for such consideration as the directors may fix. When treasury shares are disposed of for a consideration, the surplus shall be increased by the full amount of the consideration received.

(4) When reacquired shares other than converted shares are cancelled, the stated capital of the corporation shall be reduced by the amount of stated capital then represented by the shares so cancelled. The amount by which stated capital has been reduced by cancellation of reacquired shares during a stated period of time shall be disclosed in the next financial statement covering such period that is furnished by the corporation to all its shareholders, or if practicable, in the first notice of dividend or share distribution that is furnished to the holders of each class or series of its shares between the end of the period and the next such financial statement, and in any event to all its shareholders within six months of the date of the reduction of capital.

(5) Shares cancelled under this section shall be restored to the status of authorized but unissued shares, except that if the articles of incorporation prohibit the reissue of any shares required or permitted to be cancelled under this section, the board shall approve and deliver to the Registrar of Companies articles of amendment under Part IX eliminating such shares from the number of authorized shares.

43.(1) Except as otherwise provided in the articles of incorporation, the board may at any time reduce the stated capital of a corporation by eliminating from stated capital amounts previously transferred by the board from surplus to stated capital and not allocated to any designated class or series of shares, or by eliminating any amount of stated capital represented by issued shares having a par value to the extent that the stated capital exceeds the aggregate par value of such shares, or by reducing the amount of stated capital represented by issued shares without par value. If, however, the consideration for the issue of shares without par value was fixed by the shareholders under this Part V, the board shall not reduce the stated capital represented by such shares except to the extent, if any, that the board was authorized by the shareholders to allocate any portion of such consideration to surplus.

(2) No reduction of stated capital shall be made under this section unless after such reduction the stated capital exceeds the aggregate preferential amounts payable upon involuntary liquidation upon all issued shares having preferential rights in the assets plus the par value of all other issued shares with par value.

(3) When a reduction of stated capital has been effected under this section, the amount of such reduction shall be disclosed in the next financial statement covering the period in which such reduction is made that is furnished by the corporation to all its shareholders, or, if practicable, in the first notice of dividend or share distribution that is furnished to the holder of each class or series of its shares between the date of such reduction and the next such financial statement, and in any event to all its shareholders within six months of the date of such reduction.

Part VI - Directors And Management

44.(1) Subject to limitations of the articles of incorporation and of this Ordinance as to action which shall be authorized or approved by the shareholders, all corporate powers shall be exercised by or under authority of, and the business and affairs of every corporation shall be managed by, a board of directors.

(2) The directors may cause the corporation to transfer any of its assets in trust to one or more trustees, to any company, association, partnership, foundation or similar entity, and with respect to the transfer, the directors may provide that the company, its creditors, its members or any person having direct or indirect interest in the corporation, or any of them, may be the beneficiaries, creditors, members, certificate holders, partners or holders of any other similar interest.

(3) The rights or interest of any existing or subsequent creditor of the corporation in any assets of the corporation are not affected by any transfer under sub-section (2), and those rights or interests may be pleaded against any transferee in any such transfer.

45. The articles of incorporation may prescribe special qualifications for directors. Unless otherwise provided in the articles of incorporation, directors may be natural persons, or corporations, of any nationality and need not be residents of Nevis or shareholders of the corporation. Alternate or substitute directors may be appointed provided that the terms and conditions under which such appointments shall be made are set forth in the articles of incorporation or bylaws.

46.(1) The number of directors constituting the entire board shall not be less than three, except that where all the shares of a corporation are held by fewer than three shareholders, the number of directors may be fewer than three but not fewer than the number of shareholders. Subject to such limitations, such number may be fixed by the bylaws, by the shareholders, or by action of the board under the specific provisions of a bylaw. If not otherwise fixed under this section, the number shall be three.

(2) The number of directors may be increased or decreased by amendment of the bylaws, by the shareholders, or by action of the board under the specific provisions of a bylaw, subject to the following limitations:

(i) If the board is authorized by the bylaws to change the number of directors, whether by amending the bylaws or by taking action under the specific provisions of a bylaw, such amendment or action shall require the vote of a majority of the entire board; and

(ii) No decrease shall shorten the term of any incumbent director.

47.(1) At each annual meeting of shareholders, directors shall be elected to hold office until the next annual meeting except as otherwise provided in this Ordinance or in the articles of incorporation. The articles of incorporation may provide for the election of one or more directors by the holders of the shares of any class or series.

(2) Each director shall hold office until the expiration of the term for which he is elected, and until his successor has been elected and qualified.

48.(1) The articles of incorporation or the specific provisions of a bylaw adopted by the shareholders may provide that the directors be divided into either two, three or four classes. All classes shall be as nearly equal in number as possible, and no class shall include fewer than three directors.

The terms of office of the directors initially classified shall be as follows: that of the first class shall expire at the next annual meeting of shareholders, the second class at the second succeeding annual meeting, the third class, if any, at the third succeeding annual meeting, and the fourth class, if any, at the fourth succeeding annual meeting.

(2) At each annual meeting after such initial classification, directors to replace those whose terms expire at such annual meeting shall be elected to hold office until the second succeeding annual meeting if there are two classes, the third succeeding annual meeting if there are three classes, or the fourth succeeding annual meeting if there are four classes.

(3) If directors are classified and the number of directors is thereafter changed:

(i) Any newly created directorships or any decrease in directorships shall be so apportioned among the classes as to make all classes as nearly equal in number as possible; and

(ii) When the number of directors is increased by the board and any newly created directorships are filled by the board, there shall be no classification of the additional directors until the next annual meeting of shareholders.

49.(1) Newly created directorships resulting from an increase in the number of directors and vacancies occurring in the board for any reason except the removal of directors without cause may be filled by vote of a majority of the directors then in office, although less than a quorum exists, unless the articles of incorporation or the bylaws provide that such newly created directorships or vacancies shall be filled by vote of the shareholders.

(2) Unless the articles of incorporation or the specific provisions of a bylaw adopted by the shareholders provide that the board shall fill

vacancies occurring in the board by reason of the removal of directors without cause, such vacancies may be filled only by vote of the shareholders.

(3) A director elected to fill a vacancy shall be elected to hold office for the unexpired term of his predecessor.

50.(1) Any or an of the directors may be removed for cause by vote of the shareholders. The articles of incorporation or the specific provisions of a bylaw may provide for such removal by action of the board, except in the case of any director elected by cumulative voting, or by the holders of the shares of any class or series when so entitled, or by provisions of the articles of incorporation.

(2) If the articles of incorporation or the bylaws so provide, any or all of the directors may be removed without cause by vote of the shareholders.

(3) The removal of directors, with or without cause, as provided in subsections (1) and (2) is subject to the following:

> *(i)* In the case of a corporation having cumulative voting, no director may be removed when the votes cast against his removal would be sufficient to elect him if voted cumulatively at an election at which the same total number of votes were cast and the entire board, or the entire class of directors of which he is a member, were then being elected; and

> *(ii)* When by the provisions of the articles of incorporation the holders of the shares of any class or series, or holders of bonds, voting as a class, are entitled to elect one or more directors, any director so elected may be removed only by the applicable vote of the holders of the shares of that class or series, or the holders of such bonds, voting as a class.

51.(1) Unless a greater proportion is required by the articles of incorporation, a majority of the entire board present, in person or by proxy, at a meeting duly assembled, shall constitute a quorum for the transaction of business or of any specified item of business, except that the articles of incorporation or the bylaws shall not require unanimity and may fix the quorum at less than a majority of the entire board but not less than one-third thereof.

(2) The vote of the majority of the directors present in person or by proxy at a meeting at which a quorum is present shall be the act of the board unless the articles of incorporation require the vote of a greater number.

(3) A proxy shall be given in an instrument in writing including a telegram, cable, telex or similar teletransmission.

(4) Unless otherwise restricted by the articles of incorporation or bylaws, any action required or permitted to be taken at any meeting of the board of directors or of any committee thereof may be taken without a meeting if all members of the board or committee, as the case may be, consent thereto in writing and the writing or writings are filed with the minutes of the proceedings of the board or committee.

(5) Unless restricted by the articles of incorporation or bylaws, members of the board or any committee thereof may participate in a meeting of such board or committee by means of conference telephone, video, or similar communication equipment by means of which all persons participating in the meeting can hear each other, and participation in a meeting pursuant to this section shall constitute presence in person at such meeting.

(6) The articles of incorporation may contain provisions specifying either or both of the following:

(i) That the proportion of directors that shall constitute a quorum for the transaction of business or of any specified item of business shall be greater than the proportion prescribed by subsection (1) in the absence of such provision but less than the total number of directors; and

(ii) That the proportion of votes of directors that shall be necessary for the transaction of business or of any specified item of business shall be greater than the proportion prescribed by subsection (2) in the absence of such provision but less than the total number of directors.

(7) An amendment of the articles of incorporation which adds a provision permitted by subsection (6) or which changes or strikes out such a provision, shall be authorized at a meeting of shareholders by vote of the holders of two-thirds of all outstanding shares entitled to vote thereon, or of such greater proportion of shares, or class or series of shares, as may be provided specifically in the articles of incorporation for adding, changing, or striking out a provision permitted by subsection (6).

52.(1) Meetings of the board, regular or special, may be held at any place within or without Nevis, unless otherwise provided by the articles of incorporation or by the bylaws. The time and place for holding meetings of the board may be fixed by or under the bylaws, or if not so fixed, by the board.

(2) Unless otherwise provided by the bylaws, regular meetings of the board may be held without notice if the time and place of such meetings are fixed by the bylaws or the board. Special meetings of the board may be called in the manner provided in the bylaws and shall be held upon notice to the directors. The bylaws may prescribe what shall constitute notice of meeting of the board. A notice or waiver of notice need not specify the purpose of any regular or special meeting of the board, unless required by the bylaws.

(3) Notice of a meeting need not be given to any director who submits a signed waiver of notice whether before or after the meeting, or who attends the meeting without protesting the lack of notice.

53.(1) If the articles of incorporation or the bylaws so provide, the board, by resolution adopted by a majority vote of the entire board, may designate from among its members an executive committee and other committees, each of which to the extent provided in the resolution or in the articles of incorporation or bylaws of the corporation, shall have and may exercise all the authority of the board of directors, but no such committee shall have the authority as to the following matters:

(i) The submission to shareholders of any action that requires shareholders' authorization under this Ordinance;

(ii) The filling of vacancies in the board of directors or in a committee;

(iii) The fixing of compensation of the directors for serving on the board or on any committee;

(iv) The amendment or repeal of the bylaws, or the adoption of new bylaws; and

(v) The amendment or repeal of any resolution of the board which by its terms shall not be so amendable or repealable.

(2) Each such committee shall serve at the pleasure of the board. The designation of any such committee and the delegation thereto of authority shall not alone relieve any director of his duty to the corporation under this Part VI.

54.(1) No contract or other transaction between a corporation and one or more of its directors, or between a corporation and any other corporation, firm, association or other entity in which one or more of its directors are directors or officers who have a substantial financial interest, shall be either void or voidable for this reason alone or by reason alone that such director or directors are present at the meeting of the board, or of a committee thereof, which approves such contract or transaction, or that his or their votes are counted for such purpose:

> *(i)* If the material facts as to such director's interest in such contract or transaction and as to any such common directorship, officership or financial interest are disclosed in good faith or known to the board or committee, and the board or committee approves such contract or transaction by a vote sufficient for such purpose without counting the vote of such interested director or, if the votes of the disinterested directors are insufficient to constitute an act of the board as defined in this Part VI, by unanimous vote of the disinterested directors; or

> *(ii)* If the material facts as to such director's interest in such contract or transaction and as to any such common directorship, officership or financial interest are disclosed in good faith or known to the shareholders entitled to vote thereon, and such contract or transaction is approved by vote of such shareholders.

(2) Common or interested directors may be counted in determining the presence of a quorum at a meeting of the board or of a committee which approves such contract or transaction.

(3) The articles of incorporation may contain additional restrictions on contracts or transactions between a corporation and its directors and may provide that contracts or transactions in violation of such restrictions shall be void or voidable by the corporation.

(4) Unless otherwise provided in the articles of incorporation or the bylaws, the board shall have authority to fix the compensation of directors for service in any capacity.

55. A loan shall not be made by a corporation to any director unless it is authorized by vote of the shareholders. For this purpose, the shares of the director to whom the loan is to be made shall not be shares entitled to vote. A loan made in violation of this section shall be a violation of the duty to the corporation of the directors approving it, but the obligation of the borrower with respect to the loan shall not be affected thereby.

56.(1) A corporation shall have power to indemnify any person who was or is a party or is threatened to be made a party to any threatened, pending or completed action, suit or proceeding whether civil, criminal, administrative or investigative (other than an action by or in the right of the corporation) by reason of the fact that he is or was a director or officer of the corporation, or is or was serving at the request of the corporation as a director or officer of another corporation, partnership, joint venture, trust or other enterprise, against expenses (including attorneys' fees), judgments, fines and amounts paid in settlement actually and reasonably incurred by him in connection with such action, suit or proceeding if he acted in good faith and in a manner he reasonably believed to be in or not opposed to the best interest of the corporation, and, with respect to any criminal action or proceeding, had no reasonable cause to believe his conduct was unlawful.

The termination of any action, suit or proceeding by judgment, order, settlement, conviction, or upon a plea of no contest, or its equivalent, shall not, of itself, create a presumption that the person did not act in good faith and in a manner which he reasonably believed to be in or not opposed to the best interests of the corporation, and, with respect to any criminal action or proceeding, had reasonable cause to believe that his conduct was unlawful.

(2) A corporation shall have power to indemnify any person who was or is a party or is threatened to be made a party to any threatened, pending or completed action or suit by or in the right of the corporation to procure a judgment in its favor by reason of the fact that he is or was a director or officer of the corporation, or is or was serving at the request of the corporation as a director or officer of another corporation, partnership, joint venture, trust or the enterprise against expenses (including attorneys' fees) actually and reasonably incurred by him or in-connection with the defense or settlement of such action or suit if he acted in good faith and in a manner he reasonably believed to be in or not opposed to the best interests of the corporation and except that no indemnification shall be made in respect of any claim, issue or matter as to which such person shall have been adjudged to be liable for negligence or misconduct in the performance of his duty to the corporation unless and only to the extent that the court in which such action or suit was brought shall determine upon application that, despite the adjudication of liability but in view of all the circumstances of the case, such person is fairly and reasonably entitled to indemnity for such expenses which the court shall deem proper.

(3) To the extent that a director or officer of a corporation has been successful on the merits or otherwise in defense of any action, suit or

proceeding referred to in subsections (l) or (2), or in the defense of a claim, issue or matter therein, he shall be indemnified against expenses (including attorneys' fees) actually and reasonably incurred by him in connection therewith.

(4) Expenses incurred in defending a civil or criminal action, suit or proceeding may be paid in advance of the final disposition of such action, suit or proceeding as authorized by the board of directors in the specific case upon receipt of an undertaking by or on behalf of the director or officer to repay such amount unless it shall ultimately be determined that he is entitled to be indemnified by the corporation as authorized in this action.

(5) A corporation shall have power to purchase and maintain insurance on behalf of any person who is or was a director or officer of the corporation or is or was serving at the request of the corporation as a director or officer against any liability asserted against him and incurred by him in such capacity whether or not the corporation would have the power to indemnify him against such liability under the provisions of this section.

57. Directors and officers shall discharge the duties of their respective positions in good faith and with that degree of diligence, care and skill which ordinarily prudent men officers. would exercise under similar circumstances in like positions. In discharging their duties, directors and officers, when acting in good faith, may rely upon financial statements of the corporation represented to them to be correct by the president, managing director or the officer of the corporation having charge of its books or accounts, or stated in a written report by an independent public or certified public accountant or firm of such accountants fairly to reflect the financial condition of such corporation.

58.(1) Every corporation shall have:

(i) a president and treasurer, or a managing director, and

(ii) a secretary, who shall each be appointed by the board or in the manner directed by the articles of incorporation or the bylaws. Such other officers shall be appointed as are required by the articles or the bylaws or as the board may determine are desirable or necessary to carry on the business of the corporation. All officers shall be natural persons except the secretary which may be a corporation.

(2) The articles of incorporation may provide that all officers or that specified officers shall be elected by the shareholders instead of by the board.

(3) Unless otherwise provided in the articles of incorporation bylaws, all officers shall be elected or appointed to hold office until the meeting of the board following the next annual meeting of shareholders, or in the case of officers elected by the shareholders, until the next annual meeting of the shareholders.

(4) Each officer shall hold office for the term for which he is elected or appointed, and until his successor has been elected or appointed and qualified.

(5) Any two or more offices may be held by the same person unless the articles of incorporation or bylaws otherwise provide.

(6) The board may require any officer to give security for the faithful performance of his duties.

(7) All officers as between themselves and the corporation shall have such authority and perform such duties with respect to the management of the corporation as may be provided in the bylaws or, to the extent not so provided, by the board.

(8) Officers may be of any nationality and need not be residents of Nevis.

59.(1) Any officer elected or appointed by the board may be removed by the board with or without cause except as otherwise provided in the articles of incorporation or the bylaws. An officer elected by the shareholders may be removed, with or without cause, only by vote of the shareholders, but his authority to act as an officer may be suspended by the board for cause.

(2) The removal of an officer without cause shall be with out prejudice to his contract rights, if any. The election or appointment of an officer shall not of itself create contract rights.

Part VII - Shareholders

60.(1) Meetings of shareholders may be held at such place, either within or without Nevis, as may be designated in the bylaws.

(2) An annual meeting of shareholders shall be held for the election of directors on a date and at a time designated by or in the manner provided in the bylaws. Any other proper business may be transacted at the annual meeting.

(3) A failure to hold the annual meeting at the designated time or to elect a sufficient number of directors to conduct the business of the corporation shall not affect otherwise valid corporate acts or cause a dissolution of the corporation except as may be otherwise specifically provided in this Ordinance. If the annual meeting for election of directors is not held on the date designated therefor, the directors shall cause the meeting to be held as soon thereafter as convenient. If there is a failure to hold the annual meeting for a period of ninety days after the date designated therefor, or if no date has been designated for a period of thirteen months after the organization of the corporation or after its last annual meeting, holders of not less than ten percent of the shares entitled to vote in an election of directors may, in writing, demand the call of a special meeting specifying the time thereof, which shall not be less than two nor more than three months from the date of such call. The secretary of the corporation upon receiving the written demand shall promptly give notice of such meeting, or if he fails to do so within five business days thereafter, any shareholder signing such demand may give such notice.

(4) Special meetings of the shareholders may be called by the board of directors or by such person or persons as may be authorized by the articles of incorporation or by the bylaws.

(5) The articles of incorporation or the bylaws may provide that elections of directors shall be by written ballot.

61.(1) Whenever under the provisions of this Ordinance shareholders are required or permitted to take any action at a meeting, written notice to them shall state the place, date and hour of the meeting and, unless it is the annual meeting, indicate that it is being issued by or at the direction of the person or persons calling the meeting. Notice of special meeting shall also state the purpose for which the meeting is called.

(2) A copy of the notice of any meeting shall be given personally or sent by mail, telegraph, cablegram, telex or teleprinter or other written teletransmission not less than fifteen nor more than sixty days before the date of the meeting, to each registered shareholder entitled to vote at such meeting. If mailed, such notice is given when deposited in the mail directed to the shareholder at his address as it appears on the record of shareholders, or, if he shall have filed with the secretary of the corporation a written request that notices to him be mailed to some other address, then directed to him at such address.

(3) Notice of any meeting shall be given to shareholders of bearer shares in accordance with the provisions of the articles of incorporation, or the bylaws, or this Ordinance. The notice shall include a statement of the conditions under which shareholders may attend the meeting and exercise the right to vote.

(4) When a meeting is adjourned to another time or place, it shall not be necessary, unless the meeting was adjourned for lack of a quorum or unless the bylaws require otherwise, to give any notice of the adjourned meeting if the time and place to which the meeting is adjourned are announced at the meeting at which the adjournment is taken. At the adjourned meeting, any business may be transacted that might have been transacted on the original date of the meeting. However, if after the adjournment the board fixes a new record date for the adjourned meeting, a notice of the adjourned meeting shall be given to each shareholder on the new record date entitled to notice under subsection (1) of this section 61.

62. Notice of a meeting need not be given to any shareholder who submits a signed waiver of notice, in person or by proxy, whether before or after the meeting. The attendance of any shareholder at a meeting, in person or by proxy, without protest, the lack of notice of such meeting prior to the conclusion of the meeting shall constitute a waiver of notice by him.

63. Any action required by this Ordinance to be taken at a meeting of shareholders of a corporation, or any action which may be taken at a meeting of the shareholders, may be taken without a meeting if a consent in writing, setting forth the action so taken, is signed by all the shareholders entitled to vote with respect to the subject matter thereof. Such consent shall have the same effect as a unanimous vote of shareholders, and may be stated as such in any articles or documents filed with the Registrar of Companies under this Ordinance.

64. For the purpose of determining the shareholders entitled to notice of or to vote at any meeting of shareholders or any adjournment thereof, or to express consent to or dissent from any proposal without a meeting, or for the purpose of determining shareholders entitled to receive payment of any dividend or the allotment of any rights, or for the purpose of any other action, the bylaws may provide for fixing, or in the absence of such provision, the board may fix, in advance a date as the record date for any such determination of shareholders. Such date shall not be more that sixty nor less than fifteen days before the date of such meeting, nor more than sixty days prior to any other action.

65.(1) Every shareholder entitled to vote at a meeting of shareholders or to express consent or dissent without a meeting may authorize another person to act for him by proxy.

(2) Every proxy must be signed by the shareholder or his attorney-in-fact. No proxy shall be valid after the expiration of eleven months from the date thereof unless otherwise provided in the proxy. Every proxy shall be revocable at the pleasure of the shareholder executing it, except as otherwise provided in this section.

(3) The authority of the holder of a proxy to act shall not be revoked by the incompetence or death of the shareholder who executed the proxy unless, before the authority is exercised, written notice of an adjudication of such incompetence or of such death is received by the corporate officer responsible for maintaining the list of shareholders.

(4) Except when other provisions shall have been made by written agreement between the parties, the record holder of shares which are held by a pledgee as security or which belong to another, upon demand therefor and payment of necessary expenses thereof, shall issue to the pledgee or to such owner of such shares a proxy to vote or take other action thereon.

(5) A shareholder shall not sell his vote, or issue a proxy to vote to any person for any sum of money or anything of value, except as authorized in this subsection and [section 71] hereof

(6) A proxy which is entitled "irrevocable proxy" and which states that it is irrevocable, is irrevocable if and as long as it is coupled with an interest sufficient to support an irrevocable power, including when it is held by any of the following or a nominee of any of the following:

(i) A pledgee;

(ii) A person who has purchased or agreed to purchase the shares;

(iii) A creditor of the corporation who extends or continues credit to the corporation in consideration of the proxy if the proxy states that it was given in consideration of such extension or continuation of credit, the amount thereof, and the name of the person extending or continuing credit; and

(iv) A person who has contracted to perform service as an officer of the corporation, if a proxy is required by the contract of employment, if the proxy states that it was given in consideration of such contract of employment, the name of the employee and the period of employment contracted for.

(7) Notwithstanding a provision in a proxy stating that it is irrevocable, the proxy becomes revocable after the pledge is redeemed, or the debt of the corporation is paid, or the period of employment provided for in the contract of employment has terminated, and becomes revocable, in a case provided for in subsections (iii) and (iv) of paragraph (6) of this section, at the end of the period, if any, specified therein as the period during which it is irrevocable, or three years after the date of the proxy, whichever period is less, unless the period of irrevocability is renewed from time to time by the execution of a new irrevocable proxy as provided in this section. This paragraph does not affect the duration of a proxy under subsection (2) hereof

(8) A proxy may be revoked, notwithstanding a provision making it irrevocable, by a purchaser of shares without knowledge of the existence of the provision unless the existence of the proxy and its irrevocability is noted conspicuously on the face or back of the certificate representing such shares.

66.(1) Unless otherwise provided in the articles of incorporation, a majority of shares entitled to vote, represented in person or by proxy, shall constitute a quorum at a meeting of shareholders, but in no event shall a quorum consist of fewer than one-third of the shares entitled to vote at a meeting.

(2) When a quorum is once present to organize a meeting, it is not broken by the subsequent withdrawal of any shareholders.

(3) The shareholders present may adjourn the meeting despite the absence of a quorum.

67.(1) Directors shall, except as otherwise required by this Ordinance or by the articles of incorporation as permitted by this Ordinance, be elected by a plurality of the votes cast at a meeting of shareholders by the holders of shares entitled to vote in the election.

(2) The articles of incorporation of any corporation may provide that in all elections of directors of such corporation each shareholder shall be entitled to as many votes as shall equal the number of votes which, except for such provisions as to cumulative voting, he would be entitled to cast for the election of directors with respect to his shares multiplied by the number of directors to be elected, and that he may cast all of such votes for a single director or may distribute them among the number to be voted for, or any two or more of them, as he may see fit. This right, when exercised, shall be termed cumulative voting.

(3) Whenever any corporate action, other than the election of directors, is to be taken under this Ordinance by vote of the shareholders, it shall, except as otherwise required by this Ordinance or by the articles of incorporation as permitted by this

Ordinance, be authorized by a majority of the votes cast at a meeting of shareholders by the holders of shares entitled to vote thereon.

68.(1) The articles of incorporation may contain a provision specifying either or both of the following:

> *(i)* That the proportion of shares, or the proportion of shares of any class or series thereof, the holders of which shall be present in person or by proxy at any meeting of shareholders in order to constitute a quorum for the transaction of any business or of any specified item of business, including amendments to the articles of incorporation, shall be greater than the proportion prescribed by this Ordinance in the absence of such provision; and

> *(ii)* That the proportion of votes of the holders of shares, or of the holders of shares of any class or series thereof, that shall be necessary at any meeting of shareholders for the transaction of any business or of any specified item of business, including amendments to the articles of incorporation, shall be greater than the proportion prescribed by this Ordinance in the absence of such provision.

(2) An amendment of the articles of incorporation which adds a provision permitted by this section or which changes or strikes out such a provision, shall be authorized at a meeting of shareholders by vote of the holders of two-thirds of all outstanding shares entitled to vote thereon, or of such greater proportion of shares, or class or series of shares, as may be provided specifically in the articles of incorporation for adding, changing, or striking out a provision permitted by this section.

(3) If the articles of incorporation of any corporation contain a provision authorized by this section, the existence of such provision shall be noted on the face or back of every certificate for shares issued by such corporation.

69. A list of registered shareholders as of the record date, and of holders of bearer shares who as of the record date have qualified for voting, certified by the corporate officer responsible for its preparation or by a transfer agent, shall be produced at any meeting of shareholders upon request of any shareholder at the meeting or prior thereto. If the right to vote at any meeting is challenged, the inspector of election, or person presiding thereat, shall require such list of shareholders to be produced as evidence of the right of the persons challenged to vote at such meeting, and all persons who appear from such list to be shareholders entitled to vote thereat may vote at such meeting.

70.(1) Every registered shareholder as of the record date and every holder of bearer shares who, as of the record date, has qualified for voting, shall be entitled at every meeting of shareholders to one vote for every share standing in his name, unless otherwise provided in the articles of incorporation.

(2) Treasury shares are not shares entitled to vote or to be counted in determining the total number of outstanding shares.

(3) Shares of a parent corporation held by a subsidiary corporation are not shares entitled to vote or to be counted in determining the total number of outstanding shares.

(4) Shares held by an administrator, executor, guardian, conservator, committee, or other fiduciary, except a trustee, may be voted by him, either in person or by proxy, without transfer of such shares into his name. Shares held by a trustee may be voted by him, either in person or by proxy, only after the shares have been transferred into his name as trustee or into the name of his nominee.

(5) Shares by or under the control of a receiver may be voted by him without the transfer thereof into his name if authority so to do is contained in an order of the court by which such receiver was appointed.

(6) A shareholder whose shares are pledged shall be entitled to vote such shares until the shares have been transferred into the name of the pledgee, or a nominee of the pledgee.

(7) Unless otherwise provided in, and subject to, a written agreement or the bylaws or articles of incorporation, a bearer shareholder whose shares are pledged shall be entitled to vote such shares until they are delivered to the pledgee, or a nominee of the pledgee.

(8) Shares in the name of another corporation of any type or kind may be voted by such officer, agent or proxy as the bylaws of such other corporation may provide, or, in the absence of such provision, as the board of such other corporation may determine.

(9) The articles of incorporation may provide, except as limited by section 31 of Part V, either absolutely or conditionally, that the holder of any designated class or series of shares shall not be entitled to vote, or it may otherwise limit or define the respective voting powers of the several classes or series of shares, and, except as otherwise provided in this Ordinance, such provisions of such articles shall prevail, according to their tenor in all elections and in all proceedings, over the provisions of this Ordinance which authorize any action by the shareholders.

71.(1) Any shareholder, under an agreement in writing, may transfer his shares to a voting trustee for the purpose of conferring the right to vote thereon for a period not exceeding ten years upon the terms and conditions stated therein. The certificates for shares so transferred shall be surrendered and cancelled and new certificates therefor issued to such trustee stating that they are issued under such agreement, and in the entry of such ownership in the record of the corporation that fact shall also be noted, and such trustee may vote the shares so transferred during the term of such agreement. At the termination of the agreement, the shares surrendered shall be reissued to the owner in accordance with the terms of the trust agreement.

(2) The trustee shall keep available for inspection by holders of voting trust certificates at his office or at a place designated in such agreement or of which the holders of voting trust certificates have been notified in writing, correct and complete books and records of account relating to the trust, and a record containing the names and addresses of all persons who are holders of voting trust certificates and the number and class of shares represented by the certificates held by them and the dates when they became the owners thereof. The record may be in written form or any other form capable of being converted into written form within a reasonable time.

(3) A duplicate of every such agreement shall be filed in the office of the corporation and it and the record of voting trust certificate holders shall be subject to the same right of inspection by a shareholder of record or a holder of a voting trust certificate, in person or by agent or attorney, as are the records of the corporation under Part VIII of this Ordinance. The shareholder or holder of a voting trust certificate shall be entitled to the remedies provided in Part VIII of this Ordinance.

(4) At any time within six months before the expiration of such voting trust agreement as originally fixed or as extended one or more times under this section, one or more holders of voting trust certificates may, by agreement in writing, extend the duration of such voting trust agreement, nominating the same or a substitute trustee, for an additional period not exceeding ten years. Such extension agreement shall not affect the rights or obligations of persons not parties thereto and shall in every respect comply with and be subject to all provisions of this Part applicable to the original voting trust agreement.

72. An agreement between two or more shareholders, if in writing and signed by the parties thereto, may provide that in exercising any voting rights, the shares held by them shall be voted as therein provided, or as they may agree, or as determined in accordance with a procedure agreed upon by them.

73.(1) Unless otherwise provided in the bylaws, the board, in advance of any shareholders' meeting, may appoint one or more inspectors to act at the meeting or any adjournment thereof. If inspectors are not so appointed, the person presiding at a shareholders' meeting may, and on the request of any shareholder entitled to vote thereat shall, appoint one or more inspectors. In case any person appointed fails to appear or act, the vacancy may be filled by appointment made by the board in advance of the meeting or at the meeting by the person presiding thereat. Each inspector, before entering upon the discharge of his duties, shall take an oath faithfully to execute the duties of inspector at such meetings.

(2) Unless otherwise provided in the bylaws, the inspectors shall determine the number of shares outstanding and the voting power of each, the shares represented at the meeting, the existence of a quorum, the validity and effect of proxies, and shall receive votes, ballots, or consents, hear and determine all challenges and questions arising in connection with the right to vote, count and tabulate all votes, ballots or consents, determine the results, and do such acts as are proper to conduct the election or vote with fairness to all shareholders entitled to vote. Unless waived by vote of the shareholders, the inspectors shall make a report in writing of any challenge, question or matter determined by them and execute a sworn certificate of any fact found by them. Any report or certificates made by them shall be prima facie evidence of the facts stated and of the vote as certified by them.

74.(1) Except as otherwise provided in the articles of incorporation or in this section, in the event of:

> *(i)* The proposed issuance by the corporation of shares, whether or not of the same class as those previously held, which would adversely affect the voting rights or rights to current and liquidating dividends of such holders;

> *(ii)* The proposed issuance by the corporation of securities convertible into or carrying an option to purchase shares referred to in subsection (i) of this subsection; or

> *(iii)* The granting by the corporation of any options or rights to purchase shares or securities referred to in subsection (i) or (ii) of this subsection, the holders of shares of any class shall have the right, during a reasonable time and on reasonable terms to be determined by the board, to purchase such shares or other securities, as nearly as practicable, in such proportion as would, if such preemptive right were exercised, preserve the relative rights to current and liquidating dividends and voting rights of such holders and at a price or prices no less favorable than the price at which such shares, securities, options or rights

are to be offered to other holders. The holders of shares entitled to the preemptive right, and the number of shares for which they have a preemptive right, shall be determined by fixing a record date in accordance with section 64 of Part VII of this Ordinance.

(2) Except as otherwise provided in the articles of incorporation, shareholders shall have no preemptive right to purchase:

(i) Shares or other securities issued to effect a merger or consolidation;

(ii) Shares or other securities issued or optioned to directors, officers, or employees of the corporation as an incentive to service or continued service with the corporation pursuant to an authorization given by the shareholders, and by the vote of the holders of the shares entitled to exercise preemptive rights with respect to such shares;

(iii) Shares issued to satisfy conversion or option rights previously granted by the corporation;

(iv) Treasury shares; or

(v) Shares or securities which are part of the shares or securities of the corporation authorized in the original articles of incorporation and are issued, sold or optioned within two years from the date of filing such articles.

(3) The holders of shares entitled to the preemptive right shall be given prompt notice setting forth the period within which and the terms and conditions upon which such shareholders may exercise their preemptive right. Such notice shall be given personally or by mail at least fifteen days prior to the expiration of the period during which the right may be exercised.

75.(1) An action may be brought in the right of a corporation to procure a judgment in its favor, by a holder of shares or holder of voting trust certificates of the corporation or holder of a beneficial interest in such shares or certificates.

(2) In any such action, it shall be made to appear that the plaintiff is such a holder at the time of bringing the action and that he was such a holder at the time of the transaction of which he complains, or that his shares or his interest therein devolved upon him by operation of law.

(3) In any such action, the complaint shall set forth with particularity the efforts of the plaintiff to secure the initiation of such action by the board of directors or the reasons for not making such effort.

(4) Such action shall not be discontinued, compromised or settled, without the approval of the court having jurisdiction of the action. If the court shall determine that the interests of the shareholders or any class thereof will be substantially affected by such discontinuance, compromise, or settlement, the court, in its discretion, may direct that notice, by publication or otherwise, shall be given to the shareholders or class thereof whose interests it determines will be so affected; if notice is so directed to be given, the court may determine which one or more of the parties to the action shall bear the expense of giving such notice, in such amount as the court shall determine and find to be reasonable in the circumstances, and the amount of such expense shall be awarded as special costs of the action and recoverable in the same manner as statutory taxable costs.

(5) If the action on behalf of the corporation was successful, in whole or in part, or if anything was received by the plaintiff or claimant as a result of a judgment, compromise or settlement of the action or claim, the court may award the plaintiff or claimant reasonable expenses, including reasonable attorneys' fees, and shall direct him to account to the corporation for the remainder of the proceeds so received by him.

(6) In any action authorized by this section, if the plaintiff holds less than five percent of any class of the outstanding shares or holds voting trust certificates or a beneficial interest in shares representing less than five percent of any class of such shares, then unless the shares, voting trust certificates or beneficial interest of such plaintiff has a fair value in excess of one hundred thirty-five thousand dollars, the corporation in whose right such action is brought shall be entitled at any stage of the proceedings before final judgment to require the plaintiff to give security for the reasonable expenses, including attorneys' fees, which may be incurred by it in connection with such action, in such amount as the court having jurisdiction of such action shall determine upon the termination of such action. The amount of such security may thereafter from time to time be increased or decreased in the discretion of the court having jurisdiction of such action upon showing that the security provided has or may become inadequate or excessive.

Part VIII - Corporate Records And Reports

76.(1) Every corporation formed under this Ordinance shall keep correct and complete books and records of account and shall keep minutes of all meetings of shareholders, of actions taken on consent by shareholders, of all meetings of the board of directors, of actions taken on consent by directors and of meetings of the executive committee, if any.

(2) Every corporation formed under this Ordinance shall keep a record containing the names and addresses of all registered shareholders, the number and class of shares held by each and the dates when they respectively became the owners of record thereof. In addition, any such corporation which issues bearer shares shall maintain a record of all certificates issued in bearer form, including the number, class and dates of issuance of such certificates.

(3) Any of the foregoing books, minutes or records may be in written form or in any other form capable of being converted into written form within a reasonable time.

77.(1) Any shareholder or holder of a voting trust certificate, in person or by attorney or other agent, may, during the usual hours of business, inspect, for a purpose reasonably related to his interests as a shareholder, or as the holder of a voting trust certificate, and make copies or extracts from the share register, books of account, and minutes of all proceedings.

(2) Any inspection authorized by subsection (l) may be denied to a shareholder or other person who within five years sold or offered for sale a list of shareholders of a corporation or aided or abetted any person in procuring for sale any such list of shareholders or who seeks such inspection for a purpose which is not in the interest of a business other than the business of the corporation or who refuses to furnish an affidavit attesting to his right to inspect under this section.

(3) The right of inspection stated by this section may not be limited in the articles or bylaws.

78. Every director shall have the absolute right at any reasonable time to inspect all books, records, documents of every kind, and the physical properties of the corporation, domestic or foreign. of which he is a director, and also of its subsidiary corporations. Such inspection by a director may be made in person or by agent or attorney, and the right of inspection includes the right to make extracts.

79. Upon refusal of a lawful demand for inspection of records required to be maintained under this Ordinance, the person making the demand may apply to the High Court for an order directing the corporation to show cause why an order should not be granted permitting such inspection by the applicant. Upon the return day of the order to show cause, the High Court shall hear the parties summarily, by affidavit or otherwise, and if it appears that the applicant is qualified and entitled to such inspection, the High Court shall grant an order compelling such inspection and awarding such further relief as the High Court may deem just and proper. On order of the High Court issued under this section, all officers and agents of the corporation shall produce such records ordered to be produced in their custody or power, under penalty of punishment for contempt of court. All expenses of the production shall be defrayed by the applicant unless the High Court orders them to be paid or shared by the corporation.

80. Upon the written request of any person who shall have been a shareholder of record for at least six months immediately preceding his request, or of any person holding, or thereunto authorized in writing by the holders of at least five percent of any class of the outstanding shares, the corporation shall give or mail to such shareholder an annual balance sheet and profit and loss statement for the preceding fiscal year, and, if any interim balance sheet or profit and loss statement has been distributed to its shareholders or otherwise made available to the public, the most recent such interim balance sheet or profit and loss statement. The corporation shall be allowed a reasonable time to prepare such annual balance sheet and profit and loss statement.

Part IX - Amendments To Articles Of Incorporation

81. A corporation may amend its articles of incorporation from time to time in any and as many respects as may be desired, provided such amendment contains only such provisions as might lawfully be contained in the original articles of incorporation filed at the time of making such amendment.

82. Reduction of stated capital which is not authorized by action of the board may be effected by an amendment of the articles of incorporation, but no reduction of stated capital shall be made by amendment unless after such reduction the stated capital exceeds the aggregate preferential amount payable upon involuntary liquidation upon all issued shares having preferential rights in assets plus the par value of all other issued shares with par value.

83.(1) Amendment of the articles of incorporation may be authorized by vote of the holders of a majority of all outstanding shares entitled to vote thereon at a meeting of shareholders or by written consent of all shareholders entitled to vote thereon.

(2) Alternatively, any one or more of the following amendments may be approved by the board:

> *(i)* To specify or change the location of the office or registered address of the corporation; and

> *(ii)* To make, revoke or change the designation of a registered agent, or to specify or change the address of its registered agent.

(3) The articles of incorporation may be amended by consent in writing of all the incorporators provided the incorporators verify that no shares have been issued.

(4) This section shall not alter the vote required under any other section for the adoption of an amendment referred to therein, nor alter the authority of the board to authorize amendments under any other section.

84. Notwithstanding any provisions in the articles of incorporation, the holders of the outstanding shares of a class shall be entitled to vote as a class upon a proposed amendment, and in addition to the authorization of an amendment by vote of the holders of a majority of all outstanding shares entitled to vote thereon, the amendment shall be authorized by vote of the holders of a majority of all outstanding shares of the class if the amendment would increase or decrease the aggregate number of authorized shares of such class, increase or decrease the par value of the shares of such class, or alter or change the powers, preferences or special rights of the shares of such class so as to affect them adversely. If any proposed amendment would alter or change the powers, preferences, or special rights of one or more series of any class so as to affect them adversely, but shall not so affect the entire class, then only the shares of the series so affected by the amendment shall be considered a separate class for the purposes of this section.

85. The articles of amendment shall be executed for the corporation and acknowledged in accordance with the provisions of section 4 of Part I, and shall set forth:

> *(i)* The name of the corporation, and if it has been changed, the name under which it was formed;

> *(ii)* The date its articles of incorporation were filed with the Registrar of Companies;

> *(iii)* Each section affected thereby;

(iv) If any such amendment provides for a change or elimination of issued shares and, if the manner in which the same shall be effected is not set forth in such amendment, then a statement of the manner in which the same shall be effected;

(v) If any amendment reduces stated capital, then a statement of the manner in which the same is effected and the amounts from which and to which stated capital is reduced; and

(vi) The manner in which the amendment of the articles of incorporation was authorized.

The articles of amendment shall be filed with the Registrar of Companies in accordance with the provisions of section 4 of Part I.

86.(1) Upon filing of the articles of amendment with the Registrar of Companies, the amendment shall become effective as of the filing date stated thereon and the articles of incorporation shall be deemed to be amended accordingly.

(2) No amendment shall affect any existing cause of action in favor of or against the corporation, or any pending suit to which it shall be a party, or the existing rights of persons other than shareholders; and in the event the corporation name shall be changed, no suit brought by or against the corporation under its former name shall abate for that reason.

87. A holder of any adversely affected shares who does not vote on or consent in writing to an amendment to the articles of incorporation shall, subject to and by complying with the provisions of section 96 of Part X, have the right to dissent and to receive payment for such shares, if the articles of amendment *(i)* alter or abolish any preferential right of any outstanding shares having preferences; or

(ii) create, alter, or abolish any provision or right in respect of the redemption of any outstanding shares; or

(iii) alter or abolish any preemptive right of such holder to acquire shares or other securities; or

(iv) exclude or limit the right of such holder to vote on any matter, except as such right may be limited by the voting rights given to new shares then being authorized of any existing or new class.

88.(1) At any time after its articles of incorporation have been amended, a corporation may by action of its board, without necessity of vote of the shareholders, cause to be prepared a document entitled "Restated Articles of Incorporation", which will integrate into one document its original articles of incorporation (or articles of consolidation) and all amendments thereto, including those effected by articles of merger.

(2) The restated articles shall also set forth that this document purports merely to restate but not to change the provisions of the original articles of incorporation as amended and that there is no discrepancy between the said provisions and the provisions of the restated articles.

(3) The restated articles shall be executed and filed as provided in this section 85 of Part IX.

(4) A copy of the restated articles filed with the Registrar of Companies in the manner provided in section 4 of Part I shall be presumed, until otherwise shown, to be the full and true articles of incorporation as in effect on the date filed.

(5) A corporation may also integrate its articles of incorporation and amendments thereto by the procedure provided in this Part for amending the articles of incorporation.

Part X - Merger Or Consolidation

89. Whenever used in this part;

"**Merger**" means a procedure whereby any two or more corporations merge into a single corporation, which is any one of the constituent corporations;

"**Consolidation**" means a procedure whereby any two or more corporations consolidate into a new corporation formed by the consolidation;

"**Constituent corporation**" means an existing corporation that is participating in the merger or consolidation with one or more other corporations;

"**Surviving corporation**" means the constituent corporation into which one or more other constituent corporations are merged; and

"**Consolidated corporation**" means the new corporation into which two or more constituent corporations are consolidated.

90.(1) Two or more domestic corporations may merge or consolidate as provided in this part.

(2) The board of each corporation proposing to participate in a merger or consolidation shall approve a plan of merger or consolidation setting forth:

> *(i)* The name of each constituent corporation, and if the name of any of them has been changed, the name under which it was formed; and the name of the surviving corporation, or the name, or the method of determining it, of the consolidated corporation;

(ii) As to each constituent corporation, the designation and number of outstanding shares of each class and series, specifying the classes and series entitled to vote and further specifying each class and series, if any, entitled to vote as a class;

(iii) The terms and conditions of the proposed merger or consolidation, including the manner and basis of converting the shares of each constituent corporation into shares, bonds or other securities of the surviving or consolidated corporation, or the cash or other consideration to be paid or delivered in exchange for shares of each constituent corporation, or a combination thereof;

(iv) In case of merger, a statement of any amendment in the articles of incorporation of the surviving corporation to be effected by such merger; in case of consolidation, all statements required to be included in articles of incorporation for a corporation formed under this Ordinance, except statements as to facts not available at the time the plan of consolidation is approved by the board; and

(v) Such other provisions with respect to the proposed merger or consolidation as the board considers necessary or desirable.

(3) The board of each constituent corporation, upon approving such plan of merger or consolidation, shall submit such plan to a vote of shareholders of each such corporation in accordance with the following:

(i) Notice of the meeting, accompanied by a copy of the plan of merger or consolidation, shall be given to each shareholder, whether or not entitled to vote; and

(ii) The plan of merger or consolidation shall be authorized at a meeting of shareholders by vote of the holders of a majority of outstanding shares entitled to vote thereon, unless any class of shares of any such corporation is entitled to vote thereon as a class, in which event, as to such corporation, the plan of merger or consolidation shall be approved upon receiving the affirmative vote of the holders of a majority of the shares of each class entitled to vote thereon as a class and of the total shares entitled to vote thereon. The shareholders of the outstanding shares of a class shall be entitled to vote as a class if the plan of merger or consolidation contains any provisions which, if contained in a proposed amendment to articles of incorporation, would entitle such class of shares to vote as a class.

(4) After approval of the plan of merger or consolidation by the board and shareholders of each constituent corporation, the articles of merger or consolidation shall be executed in duplicate by each corporation by its president, vice president or managing director and by its secretary or an assistant secretary, and shall set forth:

(i) The plan of merger or consolidation, and, in case of consolidation, any statement required to be included in articles of incorporation for a corporation formed under this Ordinance;

(ii) The date the articles of incorporation of each constituent corporation were filed with the Registrar of Companies; and

(iii) The manner in which the merger or consolidation was authorized with respect to each constituent corporation.

(5) The articles of merger or articles of consolidation shall be filed with the Registrar of Companies in accordance with the provisions of section 4 of Part I.

91.(1) Any domestic corporation owning at least ninety percent of the outstanding shares of each class of another domestic corporation or corporations may merge such other corporation or corporations into itself without the authorization of the shareholders of any such corporation. Its board shall approve a plan of merger, setting forth:

> *(i)* The name of each subsidiary corporation to be merged and the name of the surviving corporation, and if the name of any of them has been changed, the name under which it was formed;

> *(ii)* The designation and number of outstanding shares of each class of each subsidiary corporation to be merged and the number of such shares of each class owned by the surviving corporation;

> *(iii)* The terms and conditions of the proposed merger, including the manner and basis of converting the shares of each subsidiary corporation to be merged not owned by the surviving corporation, into shares, bonds or other securities of the surviving corporation, or the cash or other consideration to be paid or delivered in exchange for shares of each such subsidiary corporation or a combination thereof; and

> *(iv)* Such other provisions with respect to the proposed merger as the board considers necessary or desirable.

(2) A copy of such plan of merger or an outline of the material features thereof shall be delivered, personally or by mail, to all holders of shares of each subsidiary corporation to be merged not owned by the surviving corporation, unless the giving of such copy or outline has been waived by such holders.

(3) The surviving corporation shall deliver duplicate originals of the articles of merger to the Registrar of Companies. The articles shall set forth;

(i) The plan of merger;

(ii) The date when the articles of incorporation of each constituent corporation were filed with the Registrar of Companies; and

(iii) If the surviving corporation does not own all the shares of each subsidiary corporation to be merged, either the date of the giving to holders of shares of each such subsidiary corporation not owned by the surviving corporation of a copy of the plan of merger or an outline of the material features thereof, or a statement that the giving of such copy or outline has been waived, if such is the case.

The articles of merger shall be filed with the Registrar of Companies in accordance with the provisions of section 4 of Part I.

92.(1) The merger or consolidation shall be effective upon the filing of the articles of merger or consolidation with the merger or Registrar of Companies or on such date subsequent thereto, consolidation not to exceed thirty days, as shall be set forth in such articles.

(2) When such merger or consolidation has been effected:

(i) Such surviving or consolidated corporation shall thereafter consistently with its articles of incorporation as altered or established by the merger or consolidation, possess all the rights, privileges, immunities, powers and purposes of each of the constituent corporations;

(ii) All the property, real and personal, including subscriptions to shares, causes of action and every other asset of each of the constituent corporations, shall vest in such surviving or consolidated corporation without further act or deed;

(iii) The surviving or consolidated corporation shall assume and be liable for all the liabilities, obligations and penalties of each of the constituent corporations. No liability or obligation due or to become due, claim or demand for any cause existing against any such corporation, or any shareholder, officer or director thereof, shall be released or impaired by such merger or consolidation. No action or proceeding, whether civil or criminal, then pending by or against any such constituent corporation, or any shareholder, officer of director thereof, shall abate or be discontinued by such merger or consolidation, but may be enforced, prosecuted, settled or compromised as if such merger or consolidation had not occurred, or such surviving or consolidated corporation may be substituted in such action or special proceeding in place of any constituent corporation;

(iv) In the case of a merger, the articles of incorporation of the surviving corporation shall be automatically amended to the extent, if any, that changes in its articles of incorporation are set forth in the plan of merger; and, in the case of a

consolidation, the statements set forth in the articles of consolidation and which are required or permitted to be set forth in the articles of incorporation of a corporation formed under this Ordinance, shall be its articles of incorporation; and

(v) Unless otherwise provided in the articles of merger or consolidation, a constituent corporation which is not the surviving corporation or the consolidated corporation, ceases to exist and is dissolved.

93.(1) One or more foreign corporations may be merged or consolidated with one or more domestic corporations in the following manner, if such merger or consolidation is permitted by the laws of the jurisdiction under which each such foreign corporation is established:

(i) Each domestic corporation shall comply with the provisions of this Ordinance with respect to the merger or consolidation, as the case may be, of domestic corporations and each foreign corporation shall comply with the applicable provisions of the laws of the jurisdiction under which it is organized;

(ii) If the surviving or consolidated corporation is to be governed by the laws of any jurisdiction other than Nevis, it shall file with the Registrar of Companies;

(1) An agreement that it will promptly pay to the dissenting shareholders of any such domestic corporation the amount, if any, to which they shall be entitled under the provisions of this Ordinance with respect to the rights of dissenting shareholders.

(2) A certificate of merger or consolidation issued by the appropriate official of the foreign jurisdiction.

(3) The effect of such merger or consolidation shall be the same as in the case of the merger or consolidation of domestic corporations if the surviving or consolidated corporation is to be governed by the laws of this jurisdiction. If the surviving or consolidated corporation is to be governed by the laws of any jurisdiction other than Nevis, the effect of such merger or consolidation shall be the same as in the case of the merger or consolidation of domestic corporations except insofar as the laws of such other jurisdiction provide otherwise.

(4) The effective date of a merger or consolidation in cases where the surviving or consolidated corporation is to be governed by the laws of any jurisdiction other than Nevis shall be determined by the filing requirements and laws of such other jurisdiction.

(5) The procedure for the merger of a subsidiary corporation or corporation under section 91 of Part X shall be available where either a subsidiary corporation or the corporation owning at least ninety percent of the outstanding shares of each class of a subsidiary is a foreign corporation, and such merger is permitted by the laws of the jurisdiction under which such foreign corporation is incorporated.

94.(1) A sale, lease, exchange or other disposition of all or substantially all the assets of a corporation, if not made in or the usual or regular course of the business actually conducted of by such corporation, shall be authorized only in accordance assets. with the following procedure:

(i) The board of directors shall approve the proposed sale, lease, exchange or other disposition and direct its submission to a vote of shareholders;

(ii) Notice of meeting shall be given to each shareholder, whether or not entitled to vote; and

(iii) At such meeting the shareholders may authorize such sale, lease, exchange or other disposition and may fix or may authorize the board to fix any or all terms and conditions thereof and the consideration to be received by the corporation therefor. Such authorization shall require the affirmative vote of the holders of two-thirds of the shares of the corporation entitled to vote thereon unless any class of shares is entitled to vote thereon as a class, in which event such authorization shall require the affirmative vote of the holders of a majority of the shares of each class of shares entitled to vote as a class thereon and of the total shares entitled to vote thereon.

(2) The board of directors may authorize any mortgage or pledge of, or the creation of a security interest in, all or any part of the corporate property, or any interest therein, wherever situated. Unless the articles of incorporation provide otherwise, no vote or consent of shareholders shall be required to authorize such action by the board of directors.

95. Any shareholder of a corporation shall have the right to dissent from any of the following corporate actions and receive payment of the fair value of his shares:

(i) Any plan of merger or consolidation to which the corporation is a party; or

(ii) Any sale or exchange of all or substantially all of the property and assets of the corporation not made in the usual and regular course of its business, including a sale in dissolution, but not including a sale pursuant to an order of a court having jurisdiction in the premises or a sale for cash on terms requiring that all or substantially all the net proceeds of sale be distributed to the shareholders in accordance with their respective interests within one year after the date of sale.

96.(1) A shareholder intending to enforce his rights under section 87 of Part IX or section 95 of Part X to receive payment for his shares if the proposed corporate action referred to therein is taken shall file with the corporation, before the meeting of shareholders at which the action is to be submitted to a vote, or at such meeting but before the vote, written objection to the action. The objection shall include a statement that he intends to demand payment for his shares if the action is taken. Such objection is not required from any shareholder to whom the corporation did not give notice of such meeting in accordance with this Ordinance or where the proposed action is authorized by written consent of shareholders without a meeting.

(2) Within twenty days after the shareholders' authorization date, which term as used in this section means the date on which the shareholders' vote authorizing such action was taken, or the date on which such consent without a meeting was obtained from the requisite shareholders, the corporation shall give written notice of such authorization or consent by registered mail to each shareholder who filed written objection or from whom written objection was not required, excepting any who voted for or consented in writing to the proposed action.

(3) Within twenty days after the giving of notice to him, any shareholder to whom the corporation was required to give such notice and who elects to dissent shall file with the corporation a written notice of such election, stating his name and residence address, the number and classes of shares as to which he dissents, and a demand for payment of the fair value of his shares. Any shareholder who elects to dissent from a merger under section 91 of Part X shall file a written notice of such election to dissent within twenty days after the giving to him of a copy of the plan or merger or an outline of the material features thereof under section 91 of Part X.

(4) A shareholder may not dissent as to fewer than all the shares that he owns beneficially. A nominee or fiduciary may not dissent on behalf of any beneficial owner as to fewer than all the shares of such owner held of record by such nominee or fiduciary.

(5) Upon filing a notice of election to dissent, the shareholder shall cease to have any of the rights of a shareholder except the right to be paid the fair value of his shares.

(6) Within seven days after the expiration of the period within which shareholders may file their notices of election to dissent, or within seven days after the proposed corporate action is consummated, whichever is later, the corporation or, in the case of a merger or consolidation, the surviving or consolidated corporation, shall make a written offer by registered mail to each shareholder who has filed such notice of election to pay for his shares at a specified price which the corporation considers to be their fair value. If within thirty days after the making of such offer, the corporation making the offer and any shareholder agree upon the price to be paid for his shares, payment therefor shall be made within thirty days after the making of such offer upon the surrender of the certificates representing such shares.

(7) The following procedures shall apply if the corporation fails to make such offer within such period of seven days, or if it makes the offer and any dissenting shareholder fails to agree with it within the period of thirty days thereafter upon the price to be paid for shares owned by such shareholder:

(i) The corporation shall, within twenty days after the expiration of whichever is applicable of the two periods last mentioned, institute a special proceeding in the High Court to determine the rights of dissenting shareholders and to fix the fair value of their shares. If, in the case of merger or consolidation the surviving or consolidated corporation is a corporation without an office in Nevis, such proceeding shall be brought in the appropriate court where the office of the corporation, whose shares are to be valued, was located;

(ii) If the corporation fails to institute such proceedings within such period of twenty days, any dissenting shareholder may institute such proceeding for the same purpose not later than thirty days after the expiration of such twenty day period. If such proceeding is not instituted within such thirty day period, all dissenter's rights shall be lost unless the Court, for good cause shown, shall otherwise direct;

(iii) All dissenting shareholders, excepting those who have agreed with the corporation upon the price to be paid for their shares, shall be made parties to such proceeding, which shall have the effect of an action quasi in rem against their shares. The corporation shall serve a copy of the petition in

such proceeding upon each dissenting shareholder in the manner provided by law for the service of a summons;

(iv) The Court shall determine whether each dissenting shareholder, as to whom the corporation requests the court to make such determination, is entitled to receive payment for his shares. If the corporation does not request any such determination or if the Court finds that any dissenting shareholder is so entitled, it shall proceed to fix the value of the shares, which for the purpose of this section, shall be the fair value as of the close of business on the day prior to the shareholders' authorization date, excluding any appreciation or depreciation directly or indirectly induced by such corporate action or its proposal. The Court may appoint an appraiser to receive evidence and recommend a decision on the question of fair value; and

(v) The final order in the proceeding shall be entered against the corporation in favor of each dissenting shareholder who is a party to the proceeding and is entitled thereto for the value of his shares so determined. Within sixty days after the final determination of the proceeding, the corporation shall pay each dissenting shareholder the amount found to be due him, upon surrender of the certificates representing his shares.

(8) Shares acquired by the corporation upon the payment of the agreed value therefor or of the amount due under the final order, as provided in this section, shall become treasury shares or be cancelled except that, in the case of a merger or consolidation, they may be held and disposed of as the plan of merger or consolidation may otherwise provide.

(9) The enforcement by a shareholder of his right to receive payment for his shares in the manner provided herein shall exclude the enforcement by such shareholder of any right to which he might otherwise be entitled by virtue of share ownership, except that this section shall not exclude the right of such shareholder to bring or maintain an appropriate action to obtain relief on the ground that such corporate action will be or is illegal or fraudulent as to such shareholder.

Part XI - Dissolution

97.(1) Except as otherwise provided in its articles of incorporation, a corporation may be dissolved if, at a meeting of shareholders, the holders of two-thirds of all outstanding shares entitled to vote on a proposal to dissolve, by resolution consent that the dissolution shall take place. A certified copy of such resolution shall be filed with the articles of dissolution.

(2) Whenever all the shareholders entitled to vote on a proposal to dissolve shall consent in writing to a dissolution, no meeting of shareholders shall be necessary. The writing or writings, or a certified copy of same, evidencing the consent shall be filed with the articles of dissolution.

(3) Articles of dissolution shall be signed and delivered to the Registrar of Companies. They shall set forth the name of the corporation, the date its articles of incorporation were filed with the Registrar of Companies, the name and address of each of its directors and officers, that the corporation elects to dissolve, and the manner in which the dissolution was authorized. The articles of dissolution shall be filed with the Registrar of Companies in accordance with the provisions of section 4 of Part I.

(4) The dissolution shall become effective as of the filing date stated on the articles of dissolution.

98. A shareholders' meeting to consider adoption of a resolution to institute a special proceeding on any of the grounds specified below, may be called, notwithstanding any provision in the articles of incorporation, by the holders of ten percent of all outstanding shares entitled to vote thereon, or if the articles of incorporation authorize a lesser proportion of shares to call the meeting, by such lesser proportion. A meeting under this section may not be called more often than once in any period of twelve consecutive months. Except as otherwise provided in the articles of incorporation, the holders of one-half of all outstanding shares of a corporation entitled to vote in an election of directors may adopt at the meeting a resolution and institute a special proceeding in Nevis for dissolution on one or more of the following grounds:

> *(i)* That the directors are so divided respecting the management of the corporation's affairs that the votes required for action by the board cannot be obtained;

> *(ii)* That the shareholders are so divided that the votes required for the election of directors cannot be obtained;

> *(iii)* That there is internal dissension and two or more factions of shareholders are so divided that dissolution would be beneficial to the shareholders;

> *(iv)* That the acts of the directors are illegal, oppressive or fraudulent; and

> *(v)* That the corporate assets are being misapplied or wasted.

If it appears, following due notice to all interested persons and hearing that any of the foregoing grounds for dissolution of the corporation exists, the High Court shall make a judgment that the corporation shall be dissolved. The registrar of the High Court shall transmit certified copies of the judgment to the Registrar of Companies. Upon filing with the Registrar of Companies, the corporation shall be dissolved.

99.(1) On the failure of a corporation to pay the annual registration fee or maintain a registered agent for a period of one year the Registrar shall remove the corporation from the register.

(2) A corporation which is removed from the register pursuant to sub-section (1) may be restored to the register within three years of the date of removal upon payment to the Registrar of the prescribed fee.

(3) A corporation shall be restored to the register retroactive to the date of its removal.

(4) Every corporation shall pay a fee for restoration to the register.

(5) A corporation which is not restored to the register within three years of the date of removal shall be deemed to have commenced to wind up and dissolve in accordance with this part.

100.(1) All corporations, whether they expire by their own limitations or are otherwise dissolved, shall nevertheless be continued for the term of three years from such expiration or dissolution as bodies corporate for the purpose of prosecuting and defending suits by or against them, and of enabling them gradually to settle and close their business, to dispose of and convey their property, to discharge their liabilities, and to distribute to the shareholders any remaining assets, but not for the purpose of continuing the business for which the corporation was organized. With respect to any action, suit, or proceeding begun by or against the corporation either prior to or within three years after the date of its expiration or dissolution, and not concluded within such period, the corporation shall be continued as a body corporate beyond that period for the purpose of concluding such action, suit or proceeding and until any judgment, order, or decree therein shall be fully executed.

(2) Upon the dissolution of any corporation, or upon the expiration of the period of its corporate existence, the directors shall be trustees thereof, with full power to settle the affairs, collect the outstanding debts, sell and convey the property, real and personal, as may be required by the laws of the jurisdiction where situated, prosecute and defend all such suits as may be necessary or proper for the purposes aforesaid, distribute the money and other property among the shareholders after paying or adequately providing for payment of its liabilities and obligations, and do all other acts which might be done by the corporation, before dissolution. that may be necessary for the final settlement of the unfinished business of the corporation.

(3) At any time within three years after the filing of the articles of dissolution, the High Court, in a special proceeding instituted under this section, upon the petition of the corporation, or of a creditor, claimant, director, officer, shareholder, subscriber for shares, or incorporator or any other person in interest, may continue the liquidation of the corporation under the supervision of the court in Nevis and may make all such orders as it may deem proper in all matters in connection with the dissolution or in winding up the affairs of the corporation, including the appointment or removal of a receiver, who may be a director, officer or shareholder of the corporation.

101.(1) Any time within one year after dissolution, a corporation may give notice requiring all creditors and claimants, including any with unliquidated or contingent claims and any with whom the corporation has unfulfilled contracts, to present their claims in writing and in detail at a specified place and by a specified day, which shall not be less than six months after the first publication of such notice. Such notice shall be published at least once a week for four successive weeks in a newspaper of general circulation in the jurisdiction which the office of the corporation was located at the date of dissolution, or if none exists, in a newspaper of general circulation in Nevis. On or before the date of the first publication of such notice, the corporation shall mail a copy thereof, postage prepaid and addressed to his last known address, to each person believed to be a creditor of or claimant against the corporation whose name and address are known to or can with due diligence be ascertained by the corporation. The giving of such notice shall not constitute a recognition that any person is a proper creditor or claimant, and shall not revive or make valid or operate as a recognition of the validity of, or a waiver of any defense or counter claim in respect of any claim against the corporation, its assets, directors, officers or shareholders, which has been barred by any statute of limitation or which has become invalid by any cause, or in respect of which the corporation, its directors, officers or shareholders, have any defense or counterclaim.

(2) Any claims which shall have been filed as provided in such notice and which shall be disputed by the corporation may be submitted for determination to the High Court. Any person whose claim is, at the date of the first publication of such notice, barred by any statute of limitations is not a creditor or claimant entitled to any notice under this section. The claim of any such person and all other claims which are not timely filed as provided in such notice except claims which are the subject of litigation on the date of the first publication of such notice, and all claims which are so filed but are disallowed by the High Court, shall be forever barred as against the corporation, its assets, directors, officers and shareholders, except to such extent, if any, as the court may allow them against any remaining assets of the corporation in the case of a creditor who shows satisfactory reason for his failure to file his claim as so provided.

(3) Notwithstanding this section, tax claims and other claims by the Government shall not be required to be filed under this Ordinance, and such claims shall not be barred because not so filed, and distribution of the assets of the corporation, or any part thereof, may be deferred until determination of any such claims.

Part XII - Transfer Of Domicile: To Nevis

102. As used in this Part, unless the context otherwise requires, the term:

"**Articles of Incorporation**" when referring to a Foreign Corporation means the articles of incorporation, certificate of incorporation, charter, statute, memorandum or other instrument defining the constitution of the corporation.

"**Corporation**" includes any incorporated organization, private law corporation, public law corporation, or similar entity.

"**Foreign Domicile**" means the seat, siege social. registered office, or any other equivalent thereto under applicable law .

"**Foreign Corporation**" means any corporation, incorporated, created or formed in any jurisdiction other than Nevis and which derives no income from operations in Nevis.

103.(1) Any Foreign Corporation may, subject to and upon compliance with the further provisions of this Part, transfer its domicile into Nevis, and may perform the acts described in the provisions of this Part, so long as the law of the Foreign Domicile do not expressly prohibit such transfer.

(2) Nothing in this Ordinance shall be regarded as permitting a foreign corporation which transfers its domicile to Nevis to transfer business operations to Nevis.

104. Any Foreign Corporation may apply for permission to transfer its domicile to Nevis by filing with the Registrar of Companies an Application to Transfer Domicile which shall be executed in accordance with section 107 of this Part and filed and recorded in accordance with section 4 of Part I of this Ordinance,

105. Said Application must contain:

(i) the date on which and the jurisdiction where the corporation was formed, incorporated created or otherwise came into existence; and

(ii) the name of the corporation; and

(iii) the foreign jurisdiction that constitutes the domicile; and

(iv) a declaration that the transfer of domicile has been approved by all necessary corporate action; and

(v) a declaration that the transfer of domicile is made in good faith and will not serve to hinder, delay or defraud existing shareholders, creditors, claimants or other parties in interest; and

(vi) the name and address of the corporation's registered agent in Nevis; and

(vii) any other pertinent information required to be set forth in articles of incorporation under Section 25 of the Ordinance; and

(viii) the amendments of its Articles of Incorporation or their equivalent, that are be effective upon filing the application to transfer domicile.

106. The Application to Transfer shall be submitted to the Registrar of Companies together with:

(i) a Certificate evidencing its corporate existence issued by an authorized officer of the Foreign Domicile; and *(ii)* a certified copy of the Articles of Incorporation, with amendments, if any, and if said documents are not in English translation thereof under oath of the translator.

107. The Application to Transfer Domicile shall be in English and notwithstanding the requirements of Section 4(3) of Part I of this Ordinance, shall be signed by any corporation officer, director, agent, trustee, manager, partner or any other person performing functions equivalent to those of any officer or director, however named or described and who is authorized to sign such Application to Transfer Domicile on behalf of the corporation.

108. Upon the filing of the Application to Transfer Domicile and the Documents referred to in Sections 105 and 106 above, together with the fees prescribed in Section 6 of Part I of this Ordinance if the Registrar of companies shall find that such documents are in proper form and satisfy the requirements of this Part, and if the name of the corporation meets the requirements of Section 22 of Part IV of this Ordinance, then the Registrar of Companies shall deliver to the corporation a Certificate of Transfer of Domicile and the corporation shall become domiciled and domesticated in Nevis as a corporation of Nevis and shall thereafter be subject to all the provisions of this Ordinance, and the corporation shall be deemed to have commenced its existence on the date the corporation was first formed, incorporated, created or otherwise came into existence and shall have continued its existence in Nevis, and thereafter. The corporation shall promptly adapt its bylaws, its registration, management and records to comply with the Nevis Law.

109. The transfer of domicile of any corporation to Nevis shall not be deemed to affect any obligations or liabilities of said corporation incurred prior to such transfer.

110. The filing of an Application to Transfer Domicile shall not affect the choice of law applicable to prior obligations and rights of the corporation, except that from the date the Application to Transfer Domicile is filed, the laws of Nevis, including the provisions of this Ordinance, shall apply to the corporation to the same extent as if the corporation had been originally incorporated as a corporation of Nevis on that date and title to the corporation's assets shall also be governed by Nevis law.

111. Any corporation formed, incorporated, created, or otherwise existing under or subject to this Ordinance may become domiciled in any foreign jurisdiction upon compliance with this Ordinance and the laws of the jurisdiction into which the corporation seeks to become domiciled.

112. Any corporation described in section 111 of this Part shall submit for filing with the Registrar of Companies a Certificate of Departure which shall be executed in the same manner as an Application to Transfer Domicile. The Certificate of Departure shall set forth:

> *(i)* The names and addresses of the corporation's creditors and the total amount of its indebtedness to such creditors, and the names and addresses of all persons or entities which have notified the corporation in writing of a claim in excess of One Thousand Dollars and the total amount of such claims; and

> *(ii)* That the intended departure from Nevis and transfer of domicile to a foreign jurisdiction is unlikely to be detrimental to the rights or property interests of any creditor of or claimant against the corporation; and

> *(iii)* That the corporation at the time of application to the foreign jurisdiction is not in breach of any duty or obligation

imposed upon it by this Ordinance or any other law of Nevis; and

(iv) That the transfer of domicile to the foreign jurisdiction is made in good faith and will not serve to hinder, delay or defraud existing shareholders or other parties in interest; and

(v) A consent and agreement by the corporation that it may be served with process in Nevis in any proceeding arising out of actions or omissions occurring prior to its departure from Nevis, which agreement shall include the appointment of the Registrar of Companies as the agent of the corporation to accept such service of process and shall set forth an address to which a copy of such process shall be forwarded by mail.

113. Upon payment of all fees outstanding in Nevis and upon proper compliance with this Ordinance and applicable laws for transfer of domicile to the foreign jurisdiction, the departing corporation shall notify the Registrar of Companies as to the effective date of the transfer of domicile outside of Nevis. As of the date of such transfer to the foreign jurisdiction, said corporation shall be deemed to have ceased to be a corporation domiciled in Nevis.

114. Nothing in this Part shall obviate, diminish or affect the jurisdiction of any court in Nevis to hear and determine any proceeding commenced therein by or against the corporation arising out of actions or omissions which occurred before the corporation ceased to be domiciled in Nevis.

Part XIII - Emergency Transfer Of Domicile Into Nevis

115. As used in this Part, unless the context requires otherwise, the term:

"**Emergency condition**" shall be deemed to include but not be limited to any of the following: War or other armed conflict; revolution or insurrection; invasion or occupation by foreign military forces; rioting or civil commotion of an extended nature; domination by a foreign power; expropriation, nationalization or confiscation of a material part of the assets or property of the corporation; impairment of the institution of private property (including private property held abroad); the taking of any action under the laws of Nevis whereby persons resident in the Foreign Domicile might be treated as "enemies" or otherwise restricted under the laws of Nevis relating to trading with enemies of Nevis; or the immediate threat of any of the foregoing; and such other event which, under the laws of the Foreign Domicile, permits the corporation to transfer its domicile.

Terms used in this Part and not defined herein are used as defined in section 102 of Part XII of this Ordinance.

116. During the existence of an Emergency Condition in the jurisdiction of its domicile, any Foreign Corporation may, subject to and upon compliance with the further provisions of this Part, apply for an emergency transfer of its domicile to Nevis.

117.(1) Any Foreign Corporation may apply for emergency transfer of domicile to Nevis by filing with the Registrar of Companies:

> *(i)* documents and certificates similar in respect to those required by sections 105 and 106 of Part XII of this

Ordinance, except that such documents shall refer to an emergency transfer of domicile pursuant to this Part XIII; and

(ii) a certificate of an authorized officer, director or agent of the corporation specifying the Emergency Condition which exists in the Foreign Domicile.

(2) The Registrar of Companies, in his discretion, may waive any of the above requirements upon request by such corporation supported by facts (including without limitation, the existence of an Emergency Condition) justifying such waiver. In addition, if Emergency Conditions have affected ordinary means of communication, any of the documents or certificates hereby required may be submitted by telegram, telex, telecopy or other form of writing so long as the duly executed original documents and supporting documentation are received by the Registrar of Companies within 30 days thereafter or as soon as the Emergency conditions cease to exist. If the Registrar of Companies finds the required documents and certificates to be in proper form upon payment of the prescribed fee, the Registrar of Companies shall certify that the corporation has filed all documents and paid all fees required by this Part, and shall deliver to the Corporation a Certificate of Transfer of Domicile, and such certificate of the Registrar of Companies shall be prima facie evidence of the transfer by such corporation of its domicile into Nevis.

118. Except to the extent expressly prohibited by the laws of Nevis after a foreign corporation transfers its domicile to Nevis pursuant to this Part XIII, the corporation shall have all of the powers which it had immediately prior to such transfer under the laws of the Foreign Domicile and the directors and officers of the corporation and their successors may manage the business and affairs of the corporation in accordance with the laws of such jurisdiction.

119. The emergency transfer by any corporation of its domicile into Nevis pursuant to this Part XIII shall not be deemed to affect any obligations or liabilities of such corporation incurred prior to such transfer.

120. All process issued out of any court of Nevis, all orders made by any court of Nevis, and all rules and notices of any kind required to be served on any corporation which has transferred it domicile into Nevis pursuant to this Part XIII may be served on the corporation and its directors pursuant to section 18 of Part III of this Ordinance in the same manner as if such corporation were a corporation of Nevis.

121. Any corporation which has transferred its domicile into Nevis pursuant to this Part XIII may return to the Foreign Domicile by filing with the Registrar of Companies a Certificate of Departure pursuant to sections 111 and 112 of Part XII of this Ordinance. Such application shall be accompanied by a certified resolution of the directors of the corporation authorizing such withdrawal.

122. Repealed.

Part XIV - Tax Exemption

123.(1) Any corporation subject to this Ordinance which does no business in Nevis shall not be subject to any corporate tax, income tax, withholding tax, stamp tax, asset tax, exchange controls, or other fees or taxes based upon or measured by assets or income originating outside of Nevis or in connection with other activities outside of Nevis or in connection with matters of corporate administration which may occur in Nevis, except as provided in sections 6 and 7 of Part I of this Ordinance.

(2) For purposes of this section, no corporation shall be considered to be doing business in Nevis solely because it engages in one or more of the following activities:

(i) maintaining bank accounts in Nevis:

(ii) holding meetings of directors or shareholders in Nevis:

(iii) maintaining corporate or financial records in Nevis:

(iv) maintaining an administrative or managerial office in Nevis with respect to assets or activities outside of Nevis:

(v) maintaining a registered agent in Nevis: and

(vi) investing in stocks or entities of Nevis corporations or being a partner in Nevis partnership or a beneficiary of a Nevis trust or estate.

(vii) acquires real property in a local industrial or tourist facility provided always that such property shall be situated in a project or development approved and authorized by the Nevis Island Administration.

Licence required for management office

123A.(1) Notwithstanding subsection (2)(iv) of section 123, no corporation shall maintain an administrative or management office in Nevis unless licensed to do so by the Minister of Finance.

(2) An application for a licence shall be in such form as may be prescribed or, until a form is prescribed, in such form as the Minister of Finance may require and shall be accompanied by such particulars and such evidence, documentary or otherwise, as the Minister of Finance requires.

(3) A licence may be issued subject to such conditions or restrictions as the Minister of Finance thinks fit to impose.

(4) A licence may be revoked by the Minister of Finance on the breach of any condition or restriction to which the licence is subject.

(5) Any corporation that maintains an administrative or management office in Nevis without a licence shall be subject to a fine of $50,000 and to be struck off the register.

(6) The provisions of this section shall apply to every corporation that -

(a) maintains an administrative or management office in Nevis immediately before the commencement of this Ordinance; or

(b) wishes to maintain an administrative or management office in Nevis on or after the commencement of this Ordinance.

(7) A corporation described in subsection (6)(a) may apply for a licence within 30 days after the commencement of this Ordinance and shall not be deemed to be in violation of this Ordinance during such period that the application is being considered by the Minister of Finance.

(8) If an application made by a corporation under subsection (7) is rejected the corporation shall close its offices in Nevis within 10 days after receipt of the notice of rejection.

Limitation of section 123A.

83B. The provisions of section 123A shall not apply to any corporation that is managed or administered by a company or a person duly licensed by the Minister of Finance in accordance with Section 17 of the principal Ordinance or in accordance with any other law enacted by the Nevis Island Legislature.

124. In addition, any dividend or distribution by a corporation which does no business in Nevis to another such corporation, or to individuals or entities which are not citizens or residents of Nevis, shall be exempt from any tax or withholding provisions of Nevis law which would otherwise be applicable to such corporation or the recipient of the dividend or distribution.

Part XV - Miscellaneous

125. This Ordinance shall not affect any cause of action, liability, penalty, or action or special proceeding which on the effective date of this Ordinance is accrued, existing, incurred or pending, but the same may be asserted, enforced, prosecuted, or defended as if this Ordinance had not been enacted.

126. Any person, natural or corporate, found in default of one or more provisions shall be liable upon summary conviction to a fine not to exceed two thousand dollars.

The Nevis International Exempt Trust Ordinance, 1994

Table Of Contents

Part 1

Preliminary

Part 2

Spendthrift, Charitable And Non-Charitable International Trusts

Part 3

Termination Or Failure Of International Trusts

Part 4

Breach Of Trust

Part 5

Powers Of The Court

Part 6

Trustees, Protectors And Beneficiaries

Part 7

Registration Of International Trusts

Part 8

Exempt From Taxes

Part 9

Miscellaneous

An Ordinance to make provision for the law relating to international trusts and for matters connected therewith.

Be It Enacted by the Queen's Most Excellent Majesty, by and with the advice and consent of the Nevis Island Assembly and by the authority of the same, as follows:

Part 1 - Preliminary

Short title

1 . This Ordinance may be cited as the Nevis International Exempt Trust Ordinance, 1994.

Interpretation

2. In this Ordinance unless the context otherwise requires -

"**bankrupt**," in relation to a corporation, includes a corporation which is insolvent, and "bankruptcy" shall be construed accordingly;

"**beneficiary**" means a person entitled to benefit under a trust, or in whose favour a power to distribute trust property may be exercised;

"**breach of trust**" means a breach of any duty imposed on a trustee by this Ordinance or by the terms of the international trust;

"**charitable purpose**" shall be construed in accordance with the provisions of section 7 of this Ordinance;

"**Court**" means the High Court of St. Christopher and Nevis;

"**creditor**" means a person to whom an obligation is owed;

"**deputy registrar**" means the person or persons appointed by the Minister to assist the registrar in performing his duties under this Ordinance;

"**formalities**" in relation to a disposition of property means documentary and other actions required generally by the laws of a relevant jurisdiction for all dispositions of like form concerning property of like nature without regard to -

(a)   the fact that the particular disposition is made in trust;

(b)   the terms of the trust;

(c)   the circumstances of the parties to the disposition; or

(d)   any other particular circumstances; but includes any special formalities required by reason that the party effecting the disposition is not of full age, is subject to mental or bodily infirmity or is a corporation;

"functions" includes rights, powers, discretions, obligations, liabilities and duties;

"the Gazette" means the Official Gazette of St. Christopher and Nevis;

"governing law" means the law governing a trust registered in Nevis or elsewhere;

"heirship rights" means any right, claim or interest in, against or to property of a person arising or accruing in consequence of that person's death, other than any such right, claim or interest created by will or other voluntary disposition or resulting from an express limitation in the disposition of the property of such person;

"insolvency" includes the making of an administration order, the appointment of a receiver and the bankruptcy of any person;

"insurance" includes assurances;

"intent to defraud" means an intention of a settlor wilfully to defeat an obligation owed to a creditor;

"interest" in relation to a beneficiary, means his interest under an international trust;

"international trust" means a trust registered under this Ordinance and in respect of which:

(a) at least one of the trustees is either:

(i) a corporation incorporated under the Nevis Business Ordinance; or

(ii) a trust company doing business in Nevis;

(b) the settlor and beneficiaries are at all times non-resident; and

(c) the trust property does not include any land situated in St. Christopher and Nevis;

"Minister" means the Minister for the time being charged with the responsibility of finance in the Nevis Island Administration;

"minor" means a person who has not attained full age under the law of his domicile;

"non-resident" means

(a) an individual not domiciled in St. Christopher and Nevis;

(b) an individual not ordinarily resident in St. Christopher and Nevis;

(c) a corporation incorporated under the Nevis Business Corporation Ordinance; or

(d) a limited liability company;

"personal representative" means the executor or administrator of the estate of a deceased person;

"**profit**" includes gain or advantage;

"**property**" -

(a) means property of any description, wherever situated, including any share therein, but excluding any land in Nevis,

(b) in relation to rights and interest, includes rights and interests whether vested, contingent, defeasible or future;

"**protector**" in relation to a trust means a person who is the holder of a power which when invoked is capable of directing a trustee in matters relating to the trust and in respect of which matters the trustee has discretion and includes a person who is the holder of a power of appointment or dismissal of trustees;

"**provisions of this ordinance**" includes the provisions of any Order hereunder;

"**registrar**" means the person appointed by the Minister to perform the duties of registrar under this Ordinance;

"**relatives**" in relation to an individual means his father and mother, his spouse, the father and mother of his spouse, his brothers and sisters, the brothers and sisters of his spouse, his children and remoter issue and the spouses of such children and issue;

"**settlor**" means a person who provides trust property or makes a testamentary disposition on trust or to a trust;

"**terms of a trust**" means the terms of an international trust, and other terms applicable under its proper law;

"trustee" has the meaning given by section 53 and includes a corporate trustee;

"trust property" means property held on trust.

Validity of international trusts

3.(1) An international trust registered under this Ordinance shall be valid and enforceable notwithstanding that it may be invalid according to the law of the settlor's domicile or residence or place of current incorporation.

(2) An international trust shall be invalid and unenforceable to the extent that -

(a) it purports to do anything contrary to the laws of St. Christopher and Nevis; or

(b) it purports to confer any right or power or impose any obligation the exercise of which or the carrying out of which is contrary to the laws of St. Christopher and Nevis.

Proper law of international trusts

4.(1) Subject to sub-section (4) below, the proper law of an international trust shall be -

(a) the law expressed by the terms of the trust or intended by the settlor to be the proper law;

(b) if no such law is expressed or intended, the law with which the international trust has its closest connection at the time of its creation;

(c) if the law expressed by the terms of the trust or intended by the settlor to be the proper law, or the law with which the

international trust has its closest connection at the time of its creation, does not provide for international trusts or the category of international trust involved then the proper law of the international trust shall be the law of Nevis.

(2) In ascertaining the law with which an international trust has its closest connection, reference shall be made in particular to -

(a) the place of administration of the trust designated by the settlor;

(b) the status of the assets of the trust;

(c) the place of residence or business of the trustee;

(d) the objects of the trust and the places where they are to be fulfilled.

(3) The terms of an international trust may provide for a severable aspect of the trust (particularly the administration of the trust) to be governed by a different law from the proper law of the trust.

(4) The terms of an international trust may provide for the proper law of the trust or the law governing a severable aspect of the trust to be changed from the law of one jurisdiction to the law of another jurisdiction.

(5) Where the proper law of an international trust or the law governing a severable aspect of an international trust is changed from the law of another jurisdiction (here called "the old law") to the law of Nevis no provision of the old law shall operate so as to render the trust void, invalid or unlawful or to render void, invalid or unlawful any functions conferred on the trustee under the law of Nevis.

(6) Where the proper law of an international trust or the law governing a severable aspect of an international trust is changed from the law of Nevis to the law of another jurisdiction (here called "the new law") no provision of the law of Nevis shall operate so as to render void, invalid or unlawful any functions conferred on the trustee under the new law.

Maximum duration of international trusts and of accumulation of income

5.(1) Subject to sub-section (2), the maximum duration of an international trust shall be one hundred years from the date of its creation and an international trust shall terminate the one hundredth anniversary of the date of its creation unless it is terminated sooner.

(2) An international trust established for a charitable or non-charitable purpose or purposes may have a duration exceeding one hundred years.

(3) The rule of law known as the rule against perpetuities shall not apply to an international trust to which this section applies.

(4) The terms of an international trust may direct or authorise the accumulation of all or part of the income of the trust for a period not exceeding the maximum duration of the trust.

Part 2 - Spendthrift Charitable And Non-Charitable International Trusts

Spendthrift trusts

6.(1) The terms of an international trust may make the interest of a beneficiary -

(a) subject to termination;

(b) subject to diminution or termination in the event of the beneficiary becoming insolvent or any of his property becoming liable to seizure or sequestration for the benefit of his creditors; or

(c) subject to a restriction on alienation of or dealing in that interest and such a trust shall be known as a protective or spendthrift trust.

(2) Where any property is directed to be held on protective or spendthrift trust for the benefit of a beneficiary, the trustee shall hold the property -

(a) in trust to pay the income to the beneficiary until the interest terminates in accordance with the terms of the trust or a determining event occurs; and

(b) if a determining event occurs, and while the interest of the beneficiary continues, in trust to pay the income to such of the following (and if more than one such shares) as the trustee in his absolute discretion shall appoint

(i) the beneficiary or any spouse or child of the beneficiary; or

(ii) if there is no such spouse or child the beneficiary and the persons who would be entitled to the estate of the beneficiary if he had then died intestate and domiciled in Nevis.

(3) In sub-section (2) above a "determining event" shall mean the occurrence of any event or any act or omission on the part of the beneficiary (other than the giving of consent to an advancement of trust property) which would result in the trust becoming payable to any person other than the beneficiary.

(4) Any rule of law or public policy which prevents a settlor from establishing a protective or a spendthrift trust of which he is a beneficiary is hereby abolished.

Charitable trusts

7.(1) For the purposes of this Ordinance and subject to sub-sections (2) and (3) below, the following purposes shall be regarded as charitable.

(a) the relief of poverty;

(b) the advancement of education;

(c) the advancement of religion;

(d) the protection of the environment;

(e) the advancement of human rights and fundamental freedoms;

(f) any other purposes which are beneficial to the community.

(2) A purpose shall not be regarded as charitable unless the fulfillment of the purpose is for the benefit of the community or a substantial section of the community having regard to the type and nature of the purpose.

(3) A purpose may be regarded as charitable whether it is to be carried out in Nevis or elsewhere and whether it is beneficial to the community in Nevis or elsewhere.

Trusts for non-charitable purposes

8.(1) An international trust may be created for a purpose which is non-charitable provided that -

    (a) the purpose is specific, reasonable, and capable of fulfillment;

    (b) the purpose is not immoral, unlawful or contrary to the public policy of St. Christopher and Nevis; and

    (c) the terms of the trust provide for the appointment of a protector who is capable of enforcing the trust and for the appointment of a successor to any protector.

(2) If the Minister has reason to believe that there is no protector of an international trust for a non-charitable purpose or the protector is unwillingly or incapable of acting, he may appoint a person to be protector of the trust and such person shall from the date or appointment exercise the functions of the trust.

Protector of a trust

9.(1) The terms of an international trust may provide for the office of protector of the trust.

(2) The protector shall have the following powers -

    (a) (unless the terms of the trust shall otherwise provide) the power to remove a trustee and appoint a new or additional trustee;

(b) such further powers as are conferred on the protector by the terms of the trust or by this Ordinance.

(3) The protector of an international trust may also be a settlor, a trustee or a beneficiary of the trust.

(4) In the exercise of his office, the protector shall not be accounted or regarded as a trustee.

(5) Subject to the terms of the international trust, in the exercise of his office a protector shall owe a fiduciary duty to the beneficiaries of the trust or to the purpose for which the trust is created.

(6) Where there is more than one protector of a trust then, subject to the terms of the trust, any functions conferred on the protectors may be exercised if a majority of the protectors for the time being agree on its exercise.

(7) A protector who dissents from a decision of the majority of protectors may require his dissent to be recorded in writing.

Part 3 - Termination Or Failure Of International Trusts

Failure or lapse of interest

10.(1) Subject to the terms of the international trust and to any order of the Court, where -

*(a)*an interest lapses;

*(b)*a trust terminates; or

*(c)*there is no beneficiary and no person (whether or not then living) who can become a beneficiary in accordance with the terms of the trust; the interest or property concerned shall be held by the trustee in trust for the settlor absolutely or, if he is dead, as if it had formed part of his estate at death.

(2) Sub-section (1) shall not apply to an international trust established for a charitable purpose to which section 11 applies.

Failure of charitable trusts

11.(1) Where international trust property is held for a charitable purpose and -

(a) the purpose has been, as far as may be, fulfilled;

(b) the purpose cannot be carried out at all, or not according to the directions given and to the spirit of the gift;

(c) the purpose provides a use for part only of the property;

(d) the purpose was laid down by reference to an area which was then, but has since ceased to be, a unit for some other purpose,

or by reference to a class of persons or to an area which has for any reason ceased to be suitable or to be practicable in administering the gift;

(e) the purpose has been adequately provided for by other means;

(f) the purpose has ceased to be charitable (by being useless or harmful to the community or otherwise); or

(g) the property and other property applicable for a similar purpose, can be more effectively used in conjunction, and to that end can more suitably be applied to a common purpose;

(h) the purpose has ceased in any other way to provide a suitable and effective method of using the property; the property or the remainder of the property, as the case may be, shall be held for such other charitable purpose, as the Court, on the application of the trustee, may declare to be consistent with the original intention of the settlor.

(2) Where international trust property is held for a charitable purpose, the Court, on the application of the trustee, may approve any arrangement which varies or revokes the purposes or terms of the trust or enlarges or modifies the powers of management or administration of the trustee, if it is satisfied that the arrangement -

(a) is now suitable or expedient; and

(b) is consistent with the original intention of the settlor.

(3) The Court shall not make a declaration under sub-section (1) above or approve an arrangement under sub-section (2) unless satisfied that any person with a material interest in the trust has had an opportunity of being heard.

Termination of international trust

12.(1) On the termination of an international trust the trust property shall, subject to sub-section (2), be distributed by the trustee within a reasonable time in accordance with the terms of the trust to the persons entitled thereto.

(2) The trustee may retain sufficient assets to make a reasonable provision for liabilities (existing, future, contingent or other).

Termination by beneficiaries

13.(1) Without prejudice to any power of the Court and notwithstanding the terms of the international trust, where all beneficiaries are in existence and have been ascertained, and none is a person under legal disability or a minor, and all beneficiaries are in agreement so to do, they may require the trustee to terminate the trust and distribute the trust property as the beneficiaries direct.

(2)A beneficiary of an interest under a protective or spendthrift trust may not enter into such an agreement as is referred to in sub-section (1).

Part 4 - Breach Of Trust

Liability for breach of trust

14.(1) Subject to the provisions of this Ordinance and to the terms of the trust, a trustee who commits or concurs in a breach of trust is liable for -

(a) any loss or depreciation in value of the trust property resulting from the breach; and

(b) any profit which would have accrued to the trust had there been no breach.

(2) A trustee may not set off a profit accruing from one breach of trust against a loss or depreciation in value resulting from another.

(3) A trustee is not liable for a breach of trust committed by another person prior to his appointment or for a breach of trust committed by a co-trustee unless -

(a) he becomes or ought to have become aware of the breach; and

(b) he actively conceals the breach, or fails within a reasonable time to take proper steps to protect or restore the trust property or to prevent the breach.

(4) Where the trustees are liable for a breach of trust, they are liable jointly and severally.

(5) A trustee who becomes aware of a breach of trust shall take all reasonable steps to have the breach remedied.

(6) Nothing in the terms of a trust shall relieve a trustee of liability for a breach of trust arising from his own fraud or wilful misconduct.

Constructive trusts

15.(1) A person who derives a profit from a breach of trust, shall be deemed to be a trustee of the profit or property, unless he derives or obtains it in good faith and without actual, constructive or implied notice of the breach of trust.

(2) A person who becomes a trustee by virtue of sub-section (1) shall deliver up the profit or property to the person properly entitled to it.

(3) This section does not exclude any other circumstance in which a constructive trust may arise.

Tracing trust property

16. Without prejudice to the personal liability of a trustee, trust property which has been charged or dealt with in breach of trust, or any property into which it has been converted, may be followed and recovered unless

(a) it is no longer identifiable; or

(b) it is in the hands of a bona fide purchaser for value without actual, constructive or implied notice of the breach of trust.

Beneficiary may relieve or indemnify trustee

17.(1) A beneficiary may relieve a trustee of liability to him for a breach of trust or indemnify a trustee against liability for a breach of trust.

(2) Sub-section (1) does not apply if the beneficiary -

(a) is a minor or a person under legal disability;

(b) does not have full knowledge of all material facts; or

(c) is improperly induced by the trustee to act under subsection (1).

Power to relieve trustee from personal liability

18. The Court may relieve a trustee wholly or partly of liability for a breach of trust where it appears to the Court that the trustee has acted honestly and reasonably and ought fairly to be excused for the breach of trust or for omitting to obtain the directions of the Court in the matter in which the breach arose.

Power to make beneficiaries indemnify

19. Where a trustee commits a breach of trust at the instigation, at the request or with the concurrence of a beneficiary, the Court (whether or not the beneficiary is a minor or a person under legal disability) may impound all or part of his interest by way of indemnity to the trustee or any person claiming through him.

20. Repealed by Ordinance No. 2 of 1995.

Part 5 - Powers Of The Court

Jurisdiction of the Court

21. The Court has jurisdiction in respect of any matters concerning an international trust where -

(a) the proper law of the trust is the law of Nevis;

(b) a trustee of the trust is resident in St. Christopher and Nevis;

(c) any part of the administration of the trust is carried on in St. Christopher and Nevis.

General powers of the Court

22.(1) On the application of a trustee, a beneficiary, a settlor or his personal representatives, a protector, or with the leave of the court, any other person, the Court may -

(a) make an order in respect of -

(i) the execution, administration or enforcement of a trust;

(ii) a trustee, including an order as to the exercise of any power by a trustee, the appointment, remuneration or conduct of a trustee, the keeping or submission of account, and the making of payment, whether into Court or otherwise;

(iii) a protector, including an order appointing a protector;

(iv) a beneficiary, or any person connected with a trust;

(v) any trust property, including an order as to the vesting, preservation, application, surrender or recovery thereof;

(b) make a declaration as to the validity of enforceability of a trust;

(c) direct the trustee to distribute, or not to distribute the trust property;

(d) make such order in respect of the termination of the trust and the distribution of the property as it thinks fit;

(e) rescind or vary an order or declaration under this Ordinance, or make a new or further order or declaration.

(2) Where the Court appoints or removes a trustee under this section -

(a) it may impose such requirements and conditions as it thinks fit, including provisions as to remuneration and requirements or conditions as to the vesting of trust property;

(b) subject to the Court's order a trustee appointed by the Court has the same functions, and may act in all respects, as if he had been originally appointed a trustee.

(3) If a person does not comply with an order of the Court under this Ordinance requiring him to do any thing, the Court may, on such terms and conditions as it thinks fit, order that the thing be done by another person, nominated for the purpose by the Court, at the expense of the person in default (or otherwise, as the Court directs) and a thing so done has effect in all respects as if done by the person in default.

Courts determination of validity

23.(1) The Court may declare an international trust to be invalid if -

(a) the trust was established by duress, mistake, undue influence or misrepresentation; or

(b) the trust is immoral or contrary to the public policy of St. Christopher and Nevis; or

(c) the terms of the trust are so uncertain that its performance is rendered impossible (provided that a charitable purpose shall be deemed always to be capable of performance); or

(d) the settlor was, at the time of its creation, incapable under the law in force in Nevis of creating such a trust.

(2) Where an international trust is created for two or more purposes of which some are lawful and others are not or where some of the terms of the trust are lawful and others are not -

(a) if those purposes cannot be separated or the terms cannot be separated, the trust is invalid;

(b) if those purposes can be separated or the terms can be separated the Court may declare that the trust is valid as to the terms which are valid and the purposes which are lawful.

(3) Where an international trust is partially invalid the Court may declare what property is to be held subject to the trust.

(4) Property provided by a settlor and as to which a trust is invalid shall, subject to any order of the Court, be held by the trustee in trust for the settlor absolutely or, if he is dead, as if it had formed part of his estate at death.

(5) In determining the existence and validity of an international trust registered under this Ordinance the Court shall apply -

(a) the provisions of this Ordinance;

(b) any other law of St. Christopher and Nevis; and

(c) any other law which may be applied; if to do so would validate the trust.

Avoidance of fraud

24.(1) Where it is proven beyond reasonable doubt by a creditor that a trust settled or established or property disposed to a trust

(a) was so settled established or disposed by or on behalf of the settlor with principal intent to defraud that creditor of the settlor; and

(b) did at the time such settlement establishment or disposition took place render the settlor insolvent or without property by which that creditor's claim (if successful) could have been satisfied, then such settlement establishment or disposition shall not be void or voidable and the international trust shall be liable to satisfy the creditor's claim and such liability shall only be to the extent of the interest that the settlor had in the property prior to settlement establishment or disposition and any other accumulation to the property (if any) subsequent thereto.

(2) In determining whether a trust, settled or established or a disposition, has rendered the settlor insolvent or without property by which a creditor's claim (if successful) may be satisfied, regard shall be had to the fair market value of the settlor's property, (not being property of or relating to the trust) at the time immediately after the settlement establishment or the disposition referred to in sub-section (1)(b) and in the event that the fair market value of such property exceeded the value of the creditor's claim, at that time, after the settlement establishment or disposition, then the trust so settled or established or the disposition shall for the purposes of this Ordinance be deemed not to have been so settled or established or the property disposed of with intent to defraud the creditor.

(3) A trust settled or established and a disposition to such trust shall not be fraudulent as against a creditor of a settlor -

(a) if settled, established or the disposition takes place after the expiration of 2 years from the date that such creditor's cause of action accrued; or

(b) where settled, established or the disposition takes place before the expiration of 2 years from the date that the creditor's cause of action accrued, that creditor fails to commence such action before the expiration of 1 year from the date such settlement establishment or disposition took place.

(4) A trust settled or established and a disposition of property to such trust shall not be fraudulent as against a creditor of a settlor if the settlement establishment or disposition of property took place before that creditor's cause of action against the settlor accrued or had arisen.

(5) A settlor shall not have imputed to him an intent to defraud a creditor, solely by reason that the settlor -

(a) has settled or established a trust or has disposed of property to such trust within two years from the date of that creditor's cause of action accruing;

(b) has retained, possesses or acquires any of the powers or benefits referred to in paragraphs (a) to (f) section 47;

(c) is a beneficiary.

(6) Where a trust is liable to satisfy a creditor's claim in the manner provided for in sub-section (1) but is unable to do so by reason of the fact that the property has been disposed of, other than to a bona fide purchaser for value, then any such disposition shall be void.

(7) For the purpose of this section the onus of proof of the settlor's intent to defraud the creditor lies on the creditor.

(8) For the purpose of this section -

(a) the date of the cause of action accruing shall be, the date of that act or omission which shall be relied upon to either partly or wholly establish the cause of action, and if there is more than one act or the omission shall be a continuing one, the date of the first act or that date that the omission shall have first occurred, as the case may be, shall be the date that the cause of action shall have accrued;

(b) in the case of an action upon a judgment, the date of the cause of action accruing shall be, the date of that act or omission or where there is more than one act or omission shall be a continuing one, the date of the first act or the date that the omission shall have first occurred, as the case may be, which gave rise to the judgment itself.

(9) The provisions of this section shall apply to all proceedings by every creditor alleging fraud against a settlor or a trust, or against any person who shall settle property upon, or dispose of property to, or establish a trust on behalf of that settlor, to the exclusion of any other remedy, principle or rule of law whether provided by statute or founded in equity or common law.

(10) In this section the term "creditor" includes any person who alleges a cause of action.

Saving of certain rights

25. In the event that a trust shall be declared invalid pursuant to this Ordinance, if the Court is satisfied that the beneficiary has not acted in bad faith -

> *(a)* the beneficiary shall have a first and paramount charge over the trust property of an amount equal to the entire costs properly incurred by him in the defense of the action or proceedings (and not merely such costs as might otherwise be allowed by the Court); and

> *(b)* the trust shall be declared invalid subject to the proper fees, costs, pre-existing rights, claims and interests of the beneficiary.

Extent of invalidity

26. An international trust shall be declared invalid only to the extent necessary to satisfy the obligation of a creditor at whose instance the trust was declared invalid together with such costs as the Court may allow.

No validation of property not vested in settlor

27.(1) Nothing in this Ordinance shall validate any disposition of property which is neither owned by the settlor nor the subject of a power in that behalf vested in the settlor.

(2) This Ordinance shall not affect the recognition of any foreign laws in determining whether the settlor is the owner of such property or the holder of such power referred to in sub-section (1) of this section.

Foreign judgment not enforceable

28. Notwithstanding the provisions of any treaty or convention; the provisions of any statute; any rule of law, or equity, to the contrary, no proceedings for or in relation to the enforcement or recognition of a judgment obtained in a jurisdiction other than St. Christopher and Nevis against -

(*a*) an international trust;

(*b*) a settlor of an international trust;

(*c*) a trustee of an international trust;

(*d*) a protector of an international trust;

(*e*) a beneficiary of an international trust;

(*f*) a person appointed or instructed in accordance with the express or implied provisions of an instrument or disposition to exercise a function or undertake any act, matter or thing in connection with an international trust; or

(*g*) property of either an international trust or of a trustee or a beneficiary thereof; shall be entertained by any Court in St. Christopher and Nevis if -

(i) that judgment is based upon the application of any law inconsistent with the provisions of this Ordinance;

(ii) that judgment relates to a matter or particular aspect that is governed by the laws of St. Christopher and Nevis.

Exclusion of foreign laws

29. No international trust governed by this Ordinance and no disposition of property to be held upon the trust shall be declared void, voidable, liable to be set aside or defective in any fashion, nor is the capacity of any settlor to be questioned by reason that: -

(a) the laws of any foreign jurisdiction prohibit or do not recognize the concept of a trust either in part or in whole; or

(b) the international trust or disposition avoids or defeats rights, claims or interests conferred by the law of a foreign jurisdiction upon any person or, contravenes any rules, law, judicial or administrative order or action intended to recognize, protect, enforce or give effect to any such rights, claims or interest; or

(c) the laws of St. Christopher and Nevis or the provisions of this Ordinance are inconsistent with any foreign law.

Applications for directions

30. A trustee may apply to the Court for directions as to how he should or might act in any of the affairs of the trust, and the Court may make such order as it thinks fit.

Payment of costs

31. The Court may order the cost and expenses of and incidental to an application to the Court under this Ordinance to be paid from the trust property or in such manner and by such persons as it thinks fit.

Part 6 - Trustees, Protectors And Beneficiaries

Beneficiaries of trusts

32. (1) A beneficiary shall be -

    (a) identifiable by name; or

    (b) ascertainable by reference to -

        (i) a class; or

        (ii) a relationship to some person whether or not living at the time of the creation of the trust or at the time which under the terms of the trust is the time by reference to which members of a class are to be determined.

(2) The terms of a trust may provide for the addition of a person as a beneficiary or the exclusion of a beneficiary from benefit.

(3) The terms of a trust may impose upon a beneficiary an obligation as a condition for benefit.

(4) A settlor or trustee of a trust may also be a beneficiary of the trust.

Disclaimer of beneficial interest

33.(1) Subject to the terms of the trust, a beneficiary may disclaim his interest or any part of it, whether or not he has received any benefit from it.

(2) A disclaimer shall be in writing and subject to the terms of the trust, may be temporary and may, if the disclaimer so provides be revoked in the manner and circumstances described or referred to therein.

(3) A disclaimer is not effective until received by a trustee.

Number of trustees

34.(1) Unless the terms of the trust provide for a greater number, the minimum number of trustees shall be one.

(2) A trust shall not cease to be valid by reason only that there is no trustee or fewer than the number of trustees required by the terms of the trust.

(3) Where there is no trustee or fewer than the number of trustees required by the terms of the trust, the necessary number of new or additional trustees shall be appointed and until the minimum number is reached the surviving trustee (if any) shall act only for the purpose of preserving the trust property.

(4) Except in the case of a trust established for a charitable purpose

(a) the number of trustees shall not be more than four; and

(b) if at any time there are more than four persons named as trustees, only the first four persons so named shall be the trustees of the trust.

Appointment of new or additional trustees

35.(1) Where the terms of a trust contain no provision for the appointment of a new or additional trustee, then -

(a) the protector (if any); or

(b) the trustees for the time being (but so that a trustee shall not be required to join in the appointment of his successor); or

(c) the last remaining trustee; or

(d) the personal representative or the liquidator of the last remaining trustee; or

(e) if there is no such person (or no such person willing to act), the Court may appoint a new or additional trustee.

(2) Subject to the terms of the trust, a trustee appointed under this section shall have the same functions and may act as if he had been originally appointed a trustee.

(3) A trustee having power to appoint a new trustee who fails to exercise such power may be removed from office by the Court.

(4) On the appointment of a new or additional trustee anything requisite for vesting the trust property in the trustees for the time being of the trust shall be done.

Corporate trustees

36. A corporate trustee may -

*(a)*act in connection with a trust by resolution of the corporate trustee or of its board of directors or other governing body; or

*(b)*NEVIS OFFSHORE BANKING ORDINANCE 1996

Preliminary

Short title

1. This Ordinance may be cited as the Nevis Offshore Banking Ordinance, 1996.

Interpretation

2. In this Ordinance

"auditor" means an auditor described in section 43 and includes a partnership of auditors.

"business" in relation to a licensee means offshore banking business of the licensee;

"director," means a director within the meaning of section 32;

"licensee" means a body corporate that holds a subsisting licence under this Ordinance to carry on an offshore banking business from within Nevis;

"Minister" means the Minister responsible for Finance in the Nevis Island Administration;

"offshore banking" has the meaning given that expression in section 4;

"permanent secretary" means the permanent secretary in the Ministry of Finance in the Nevis Island Administration;

"prescribed" means prescribed by regulations;

"share" in relation to a company includes stock of the company.

(2) A reference in this Ordinance to a resident of Nevis refers to a person described in section 86, and a reference to a person resident outside Nevis refers to a person described in section 87.

Purposes of Ordinance

3.(1) The purposes of this Ordinance are

>   *(a)* to encourage the development of Nevis as a responsible offshore financial centre;

(b) to provide incentives by way of tax reduction, exemptions and benefits for offshore banking carried on from within Nevis; and

(2) This Ordinance shall receive such fair and liberal construction interpretation as will best ensure the attainment of its purposes.

Part I - Offshore Banking

Offshore banking

4.(1) Offshore banking is

(a) receiving foreign funds through

(i) the acceptance of foreign money deposits payable upon receipt demand or after a fixed period or after notice,

(ii) the sale or placement of foreign bonds, certificates, notes or other debt obligations or other securities, or

(iii) any other similar activities involving foreign money or foreign securities, and

(b) either in whole or in part using foreign funds so acquired for loans, advances and investments whether in Nevis or elsewhere.

(2) Offshore banking also includes, for the purpose of this Ordinance, any other activity, which the minister may, by regulations, declare to be an activity related or ancillary to an activity described in subsection (1).

Prohibition without licence

5. No person shall engage in offshore banking in or from within Nevis at any time when he is not a licensee.

Issue of licences.

6. No licence may be issued under this Ordinance to any person other than an eligible company or qualified foreign bank.

Eligible company

7.(1) A body corporate is an eligible company if it is a wholly owned subsidiary of a local bank regulated by the Eastern Caribbean Central Bank that is licensed under the Banking Act to do banking business in Nevis.

(2) For the purposes of subsection (1) a local bank means a bank indigenous to St. Kitts and Nevis.

Qualified foreign bank

8. A qualified foreign bank is

(a) a foreign bank that upon the commencement of this Ordinance is licensed under the Banking Act,

(b) a foreign bank with minimum capitalisation and assets, as prescribed by the Minister, that is not licensed under the Banking Act but is licensed to do domestic banking in its jurisdiction of incorporation,

(c) a financial institution, approved by the Minister, that is directly or indirectly a wholly owned foreign subsidiary within the meaning of section 13(6), of a foreign bank described in paragraph (a) or (b) above.

Part II - Licensing Requirements

Consent of Minister

9.(1) Notwithstanding the Companies Act, no company may be incorporated under that Act for the purpose of doing offshore banking from within Nevis unless its incorporation has or been consented to by the Minister.

(2) Notwithstanding anything in its memorandum or articles of association, no company incorporated under the Companies Act before the commencement of this Ordinance has capacity to do offshore banking from within Nevis unless its memorandum and articles of association are, or are amended, to the satisfaction of the Minister.

Application requirements

10.(1) An eligible company must

(a) be incorporated under the Companies Act as a company limited by shares,

(b) have objects or business activities restricted to off-shore banking from within Nevis,

(c) have at least one director who is a citizen of St. Kitts and Nevis with a residence in Nevis;

(d) have memorandum and articles of association acceptable to the Minister,

(e) have authorised and paid up capital in accordance with the requirements of section 22.

(2) Every applicant for a licence under this Ordinance must *(a)* show that it is an eligible company or a qualified foreign bank,

(b) give the names and address of its directors,

(c) give particulars of the off-shore banking it proposes to do from within Nevis,

(d) give the names of any shareholders who are residents of Nevis and the number of shares held directly or indirectly by residents of Nevis, and

(e) provide such other information of a financial or other nature as the Minister may require in any particular case.

(3) An application for a licence by an eligible company must be accompanied by a certified copy of the memorandum and articles of association of the applicant.

(4) An application for a licence and all documents submitted pursuant to this Ordinance in support of the application must be signed by the directors of the company making the application.

(5) An application for a licence by a qualified foreign bank must be accompanied by such documents as are prescribed by the Minister.

Tentative applicants

11.(1) Any person who intends to apply for a licence under this Ordinance may submit a proposal to the Minister for a licence, and the Minister may indicate whether or not a subsequent application based on the proposal would be favourably received by him.

(2) Nothing done by the Minister under subsection (1) precludes him from later refusing an application for a licence that was based on a proposal considered by him pursuant to that section on grounds that the applicant withheld material information or that the proposed application was made in bad faith.

Director's qualification

12. Where a company has appointed a citizen of St. Kitts and Nevis who is a resident of Nevis to its board of directors under this Ordinance, that director need not subscribe for nor acquire any shares of the company.

Examination of applicants

13.(1) On receipt of an application for a licence under this Ordinance, the Minister may cause such investigation to be made of the applicant, its financial circumstances, and any associates or affiliates of the applicant, as the Minister considers necessary in the public interest.

(2) In particular, the Minister shall require an examination to be made of

(a) the financial status and history of the applicant and any of its directors associates or affiliates,

(b) the character and experience of the directors thereof,

(c) the adequacy of its capital for the purpose of the business it intends to carry on,

(d) the needs of the public or persons it intends to serve, and

(e) its earning prospects and its prospects as an employer.

(3) For the purposes of this section, "associate" means, when used to indicate a relation with any person

(a) a company of which that person beneficially owns or controls, directly or indirectly, shares or securities convertible into shares carrying more than ten per cent of the voting rights under all

circumstances or by reason of occurrence of an event that has occurred and is continuing, or a currently exercisable option or right to purchase those shares or convertible securities;

(b) a partner of that person acting on behalf of the partnership of which they are partners;

(c) a trust or estate in which that person has a substantial beneficial interest or in respect of which he serves as a trustee or in a similar capacity;

(d) a spouse or a child of that person; or

(e) a relative of that person or of the spouse of that person if the relative has the same residence as that person.

(4) For the purpose of this section

(a) one company is affiliated with another company if one of them is the subsidiary of the other or both are subsidiaries of the same holding company or each of them is controlled by the same person;

(b) if two companies are affiliated with the same company at the same time, they are affiliated with each other at that time.

(5) A company is the holding company of another if that other company is its subsidiary.

(6) A company is a subsidiary of another company if it is controlled by that other company.

Duty to issue or refuse licence

14.(1) It is the duty of the Minister to issue or refuse a licence under this Ordinance to an applicant.

(a) within three months of the receipt of the application, or

(b) if additional information is required by the Minister, within fourteen days of the receipt by him of that additional information.

(2) When the Minister is of the opinion that it is in the public interest to do so, he may issue a licence under this Ordinance to the applicant upon payment of the prescribed fee.

Licence and conditions

15.(1) A licence issued under this Ordinance must show the kinds of off-shore banking to be done from within Nevis by the licensee.

(2) A licence under this Ordinance is subject to such conditions as the Minister may specify in respect of the offshore banking to be done by the licensee from within Nevis.

(3) A licence under this Ordinance remains valid until revoked pursuant this Ordinance but it is a condition of every licence that an annual fee be paid by every class of licensee in the amount and at the time prescribed.

(4) It is a condition of a licence under this Ordinance that the licensee will notify the Permanent Secretary of the creation by it of any subsidiary company within the meaning of section 13 and that it will notify the Permanent Secretary whenever it opens a place of business outside Nevis.

(5) Subsection (4) does not apply to a licensee that is a qualified foreign bank but the licensee shall not, without notifying the Permanent Secretary of its intention to do so, create any subsidiary company within the meaning of section 13 to carry on offshore banking from within Nevis.

Other special conditions

16. (1) It is a condition of a licence under this Ordinance that

(a) any voting shares of the licensee's capital will be in registered form;

(b) the licensee will not, without the approval of the Minister;

(i) enter into a merger, amalgamation or consolidation,

(ii) transfer, otherwise than in the ordinary course of its business, the whole or any substantial part of its assets or liabilities,

(iii) change its name from that set out in its licence,

(iv) alter its memorandum or articles of association, or

(v) transfer any of its shares;

(c) the licensee will not knowingly in the course of its business accept any deposit for the account of a resident of Nevis or keep a resident of Nevis as a customer for any of its offshore banking services, or

(d) the licensee that is a qualified foreign bank will, in the manner and to the extent prescribed, separate offshore banking activities from its other activities in Nevis and keep separate records of its offshore banking activities and will permit and assist in an audit of all its undertakings in Nevis by auditors approved by the Minister.

(2) Before giving an approval to any matter mentioned in subsection (1) the Minister shall carry out such of the investigations specified in section 13 as he thinks required.

(3) Paragraphs (a) and (b) of subsection (1) and subsection (2) do not apply to a licensee that is a qualified foreign bank.

Display of licence

17. A licensee shall display in a conspicuous place at each place where it does business a copy of its current licence under this Ordinance.

Revocation of licence

18.(1) The Minister may revoke a licence if the licensee

(a) does not within six months after the issuance of its licence commence business;

(b) fails to comply with a condition of its licence;

(c) is in breach of any duty or obligation imposed upon it by this Ordinance or commits an offence under this Ordinance; or

(d) ceases to carry on business under its licence.

(2) When the Minister intends to revoke a licence under subsection (1) it is his duty to give the licensee notice of his intention and a reasonable opportunity to show cause why the licence should not be revoked.

(3) The Minister must give notice in writing to the licensee of the revocation of the licence.

Right of appeal

19.(1) Any person who is aggrieved by the revocation of a licence by the Minister under section 18 may, within twenty-one days of the giving of the notice under section 18(3), appeal the revocation to a judge of the High Court, in chambers, whose decision thereon is final.

(2) Where the Minister revokes a licence and there is no appeal or where there is an appeal and the appeal is disallowed, the notice of the revocation must be published in the Gazette and in a newspaper of general circulation in Nevis.

Misleading name

20. No licensee may be granted a licence under a name of an existing bank trust company or other company carrying on business in Nevis or elsewhere as would in the opinion of the Minister mislead or confuse the persons for whom it intends to provide any or all of its services.

Service on licensee

21.(1) Before it does any offshore banking from within Nevis a licensee must deposit with the Permanent Secretary

> *(a)* a duly executed instrument that appoints the Permanent Secretary as its agent for the acceptance of service of documents in any action arising out of the operations of the licensee; and

> *(b)* a certificate setting out the name and address of any person in Nevis to whom documents related to the licensee and served on the Permanent Secretary are to be forwarded.

(2) It is the duty of the Permanent Secretary to ensure that all process, instruments and other documents served on him pursuant to subsection (1) in respect of a licensee are forwarded within ten days to the person named in a certificate described in paragraph (1) (b) in the case of that licensee.

Financial obligation

22.(1) A licence may be issued under this Ordinance to an eligible company when

(a) the authorised capital of the company is at least two million dollars; and

(b) capital to an amount of not less than one million dollars has been subscribed and paid-up in cash, such cash shall be deposited in an account maintained by the Permanent Secretary at the Eastern Caribbean Central Bank.

(2) For the purposes of this section and section 13, a licensee is controlled by another company or by an individual or government, if at the relevant time it is effectively controlled directly or indirectly by that other company, individual or government

(a) through being an associate within the meaning of section 13 of that other company, individual or government;

(b) through being an affiliate within the meaning of section 13 of that other company;

(c) through the holding of shares of an incorporated body, but subject to subsection (4);

(d) through the holding of membership in an unincorporated body;

(e) through voting trusts or other agreements relating to the voting of shares;

(f) through the holding by an unincorporated body of a substantial portion of the licensee's borrowings;

(g) through management control of an unincorporated body; or

(h) through any other similar means.

(4) A company is controlled by a person if shares of the company that carry voting rights sufficient to elect a majority of the directors of the company are held, directly, other than by way of security only, by or on behalf of that person.

(5) Whether or not any licensee is effectively controlled directly or indirectly by persons who are residents of Nevis is a question of fact determinable by the Minister whose decision thereon is final for the purposes of this Ordinance.

Reserves

23.(1) Subject to subsection (2), a licensee shall maintain a reserve fund and shall out of its net profits of each year and before any dividend is paid transfer to the fund a sum equal to not less than twenty-five per cent of those profits whenever the amount of the reserve fund is less than the paid-up capital of the licensee.

(2) Subsection (1) does not apply to a licensee for whom it is shown to the satisfaction of the Minister that the aggregate reserves of the licensee are adequate in relation to its business.

Dividends

24. A licensee shall not declare or pay a dividend if there are reasonable grounds for believing that

(a) the licensee is, or would after the payment be, unable to pay its liabilities as they become due, or

(b) the realizable value of the licensee's assets would thereby be less than the aggregate of its liabilities and capital.

Part III - Abandoned Property

Abandoned property

25.(1) Property of the following kinds held or owing in the course of its business by a licensee in respect of which no activity has been evidenced for a period of ten years is abandoned property:

> *(a)* any general deposit, that is a demand saving or matured time deposit made with the licensee together with any interest or dividends but exclusive of legal charges;

> *(b)* funds that were paid towards the purchase of shares or other interests in a licensee;

> *(c)* any sum payable on cheques or other instruments on which the licensee is liable; and in respect of which the licensee has, by registered mail to the latest known address of the lessee, given notice of its intention to deliver the contents into the custody of the Nevis Island Administration and the lessee has failed to respond within a period of one year.

(2) Activity is evidenced in respect of the property described in subsection (1) if the owner thereof has

> *(a)* within ten years of the date of deposit increased or decreased the amount of the deposit or presented a passbook or other record for the crediting of interest in respect of the deposit;

> *(b)* within ten years of paying funds for the purchase of shares or other interest mentioned in subsection (l)(b), increased or decreased the amount of the funds or presented a document or book for crediting of dividends in respect thereof;

(c) within ten years of making the last deposit, inquiry or communication concerning any item mentioned in subsection (1), corresponded with the licensee concerning the items or otherwise indicated an interest in the items as evidenced by a memorandum about them by the licensee.

Disposal of abandoned property

26.(1) A licensee shall, once in each financial year, report to the Permanent Secretary all its holding of abandoned property within the meaning of this Ordinance and shall, from time to time, deposit with or convey to the Nevis Island Administration in the prescribed manner all abandoned property.

(2) When a licensee has deposited with or conveyed to the Nevis Island Administration any abandoned property, the licensee is relieved from any liability to the beneficial owners thereof to the extent of the value of the property deposited or conveyed to the Nevis Island Administration.

(3) Within thirty days after reporting to the Permanent Secretary pursuant to subsection (1), the Permanent Secretary shall give notice by registered mail to the beneficial owner of the property, at his latest known address; but with the approval of the High Court on application thereto, the Permanent Secretary may be exempted from mailing the copy of the notice to the owner.

Sale of abandoned property

27.(1) The Nevis Island Administration may sell at public auction any property that has been conveyed to it under section 26 after the expiration of thirty days from the latest of the date of publication of the notice referred to in section 26(3) and the mailing of the copy of the notice to the owner, as the case may be.

(2) The public auction may be held after such reasonable advertising of the sale as the Nevis Island Administration considers suitable.

Payment to Consolidated Fund

28. The Permanent Secretary shall pay into the Nevis Island Consolidated Fund all money received by the Nevis Island Administration as abandoned property and the proceeds of the public auction of any abandoned property less, in each case

(a) such amount as the Minister considers necessary to reserve for the payment of claims later made and approved by him; and

(b) amounts deducted by the Permanent Secretary as approved by the Minister for reasonable expenses incurred in connection with the publishing and mailing of notice, service charges, and the sale of abandoned property.

Claims against property

29.(1) A person who claims a beneficial interest in any abandoned property deposited with or conveyed to the Nevis Island Administration may make a claim for the value thereof within the prescribed time and in the prescribed manner.

(2) When the Minister is satisfied that a claimant is entitled to the abandoned property, the Nevis Island Administration shall deliver up the property, or make payment for the value thereof, as the case requires.

Notice to claimants

30.(1) When the Minister admits or refuses a claim under section 29, he shall forthwith notify the claimants of his decision.

(2) A person aggrieved by a refusal of his claim for abandoned property by the Minister may within twenty-one days of receiving notice of the refusal, appeal the decision to a judge of the High Court in chambers who may make such order thereon as he considers equitable.

Offence re abandoned property

31. A licensee that fails to report to the Permanent Secretary any abandoned property in its possession or that fails to deposit with or convey to the Nevis Island Administration any abandoned property as required by this Ordinance, is guilty of an offence and liable on summary conviction to a fine not exceeding twenty five thousand dollars.

Part IV - Administration Of Licensees

Director

32. For the purpose of this Ordinance,

(a) "**director**" means an individual occupying the like position and performing the like functions of a director under the Companies Act, however his position is designated.

*(b)*a reference to "**directors**" refers to the board of directors or the body directing the affairs of a company or firm.

Office of director

33. A director of a licensee cease to hold office as a director thereof

(a) if he becomes bankrupt or suspends payment to his creditors;

(b) if he is convicted in Nevis of an offence triable on indictment; or

(c) if he is convicted outside Nevis of an offence that would be triable on indictment had it been committed in Nevis;

(d) if he becomes of unsound mind.

Disqualification of director

34. A person who has been a director of a licensee whose licence is revoked under this Ordinance shall not, without the prior approval of the Minister act or continue to act as a director of any other licensee.

Disclosure of interest

35.(1) A director of a licensee who is interested, directly or indirectly in an advance or loan from the licensee shall as soon as possible declare the nature of his interest to its directors at a meeting thereof.

(2) Subsection (1) does not apply when the interest of a director in an advance or loan consists only of being a creditor of or having an interest in a firm that is interested in an advance or loan from the licensee if, in either case, the interest of the director is not a substantial interest.

(3) A declaration by a director of a licensee that he is interested in any advance or loan that may, after the date of the declaration, be made by the licensee is a sufficient declaration of interest in relation to any advance or loan made after the declaration, if

(a) the declaration specified the nature and extent of the interest; and

(b) the interest of the director is not different in nature from, or greater than, the nature and extent so specified in the declaration at the time any advance or loan is made.

Declaration of interest

36.(1) A director of a licensee who holds any office or has any interest in any property whereby, directly or indirectly, his functions under this Ordinance are likely to be in conflict with his personal interests shall declare the nature, character and extent of that office or interest to the directors at a meeting thereof.

(2) A declaration required under this section shall be made *(a)* at the first meeting of the directors that is held after the acquisition by the declarant of that relevant office or interest, or

(b) if the declarant was not at that time a director, after he becomes a director.

(3) A director to whom this section or section 35 applies shall in any event notify the Secretary of the licensee of his interest so that the Secretary may convene a meeting of the Board of Directors for the purpose of considering the declaration, unless a meeting of the Board of Directors is already scheduled to be held within 14 days following the receipt of notification by the Secretary of the Director's declaration.

Recording declaration

37. A director of a licensee who has declared any interest referred to in section 35 or 36 shall

(a) cause the declaration made by him thereunder to be brought up and read at the next meeting of the directors after it was given; and

(b) cause the declaration to be recorded in the minutes of the meeting at which it was made or read or both.

Offence

38. A director of a licensee who contravenes section 34, 35 or 36 is guilty of an offence and liable on conviction to a fine not exceeding five thousand dollars or to imprisonment for twelve months or to both.

Insider information

39.(1) A person who has acquired confidential information concerning a licensee

    (a) as a director, officer, employee or auditor of the licensee,

    (b) as a custodian of the licensee, or

    (c) as an employee of the Nevis Island Administration shall not disclose that information to any person except as permitted under subsection (2) or use that information for any personal benefit not related to the duties through which the information was acquired.

(2) Subsection (1) does not apply to the giving of confidential information

    (a) when the information is a general credit rating of a person that is supplied by a director, officer or employee of the licensee following a bona fide business request;

    (b) when the information is given with the written authorization of the beneficiary or his legal representative;

    (c) when the information is lawfully required to be disclosed by an order of the High Court, or

    (d) when the information is lawfully disclosed pursuant to any other enactment.

(4) In this section "confidential information" means information concerning the identity of a depositor or concerning the assets, liabilities, transactions or other information in respect of a depositor.

Part V - Audit And Inspection

Financial Statements

40.(1) A licensee shall, in respect of its business, submit to the Permanent Secretary in prescribed form

> *(a)* not later than twenty-one days after the end of each three month period, a quarterly statement of the assets and liabilities of the licensee; and

> *(b)* within such time as the Minister may determine, such other returns as the Permanent Secretary requires

(2) The Minister may require a licensee to submit such further information as he considers necessary for the proper understanding of any statement or return furnished by the licensee pursuant to subsection (1) and the further information shall be submitted within such time and in such manner as the Minister requires.

Confidentiality

41.(1) No statement, return or information shall be required by the Permanent Secretary or the Minister with respect to the affairs of any particular offshore banking customer of a licensee, but the Minister may seek and be informed of the names of any residents of Nevis who are customers of the licensee.

(2) No statement, returns or information furnished or submitted by a licensee in respect of its business shall be communicated or disclosed except to the Minister and such public officers and other persons as may be prescribed.

Publication of balance sheets

42.(1) Not later than four months after the close of its financial year or such longer period as the Minister may allow, a licensee shall forward to the Permanent Secretary copies of its balance sheet and profit and loss account and the full and correct names of the directors of the licensee.

(2) The balance sheet and the profit and loss account must bear on its face the certificate of an auditor.

Auditor

43. In this Ordinance, unless the context otherwise requires-

"**auditor**" means a person who

> *(a)* is qualified as an accountant by examination of, one of the institutes of Chartered Accountants or Certified Accountants in England and Wales, Ireland or Scotland, the Canadian Institute of Chartered Accountants or the American Institute of Certified Public Accountants and holds a current practising certificate if required by his institute to do so; or

> *(b)* possesses such other qualification in accountancy, banking or other similar qualification equivalent to the qualification set forth in paragraph (a) as the Minister may, by order, approve and is in good standing with respect to such qualification.

Annual auditing

44.(1) The annual balance sheets, and accounts of a licensee shall be audited at least once in every financial year by an auditor appointed by the licensee from a list of auditors maintained by the Permanent Secretary.

(2) It is the duty of the auditor appointed pursuant to subsection (1) to submit a report to the shareholders of the licensee and to the Permanent Secretary.

(3) The report of the auditor shall state whether the auditor has obtained all the information and explanations he needed and in addition state whether in his opinion the balance sheet and accounts exhibit a true and correct view of the assets and liabilities of the licensee as at the date of the statement, and the income and expenditure of the licensee for the year then ended.

(4) It is the duty of the auditor to note in his report any instances where the operations of the licensee might not in the opinion of the auditor be in compliance with the requirements of this Ordinance or any regulations made hereunder, the conditions of the licensee's licence or its memorandum or articles of association.

(5) The report of the auditor shall be read with the report of the directors to the shareholders at the annual meeting of the licensee.

(6) A copy of the report of the auditor shall be displayed by the licensee in a conspicuous place at its office in Nevis.

(7) If the Permanent Secretary has reasonable grounds for not being satisfied with the annual report of an auditor appointed by a licensee, the Permanent Secretary may appoint another auditor to make an independent report.

(8) When a licensee fails to appoint an auditor pursuant to this section, the Permanent Secretary may appoint an auditor who has all the powers of an auditor appointed by the licensee to carry out an audit.

(9) The remuneration of an auditor shall be paid by the licensee to which he is appointed and, if the auditor is appointed under subsection (7) or (8), his remuneration shall be such amount as the Minister determines.

Prohibited auditors

45. No person may be appointed an auditor of a licensee

(a) if he has any proprietary interest in the licensee,

(b) if he is a director, or agent of the licensee or of an affiliate of the licensee, within the meaning of section 13; or

(c) if he is an officer or employee of the Nevis Island Administration.

Examination by Minister

46.(1) When the Minister has reasonable grounds to believe that a licensee is not in a sound financial condition or that it is not acting in compliance with this Ordinance, the Minister may apply to the High Court for an order to examine the affairs of the licensee.

(2) The High Court may, having regard to the purposes of this Ordinance, grant an application under subsection (1) subject to such conditions as the High Court considers appropriate in all the circumstances.

(3) When the High Court grants an application under subsection (2) the Minister shall appoint a fit and proper person to examine the licensee.

Powers of examiners

47.(1) Subject to subsection (2), a licensee shall produce for an examiner appointed under section 46 by the Minister at such time as the examiner fixes, all books, minutes, cash, securities, vouchers and other documents and records relating to its assets, liabilities and business generally and shall give the examiner such information concerning its affairs and business as he may request.

(2) An examiner may not have access to, nor shall he be given access to, the name or the account of any depositor if the depositor is not a resident of Nevis.

Access by court order

48. Notwithstanding section 47 (2), the High Court may, on the application of the Minister, order the production of information protected under that section if the court is satisfied that it is required in the public interest by the examiner for the proper performance of his functions under this Ordinance and that there are no other lawful means of acquiring the information.

Offence and penalty

49. If any of the matters referred to in section 47 are not produced, or the information relating thereto is not given, to the examiner by the licensee, the licensee is guilty of an offence and liable on summary conviction to a fine of five thousand dollars and in addition, to a further fine of five hundred dollars for each day during which the offence continues.

Remedial action

50.(1) When the Minister is of the opinion that an examination of a licensee indicates that the licensee is carrying on its business in an unlawful manner or is an unsound financial condition, the Minister may

> *(a)* require that the licensee immediately take such remedial measures as he considers necessary; and

(b) appoint a person who in his opinion has had training and experience in the business of the licensee concerned, to advise the licensee on the action to be taken to remedy the situation, or

(c) suspend the licence of the licensee for a period not exceeding three months.

(2) A person appointed under subsection (1)(b) shall be paid by the Nevis Island Administration such remuneration as the Minister may determine, which remunerationshall be charged to the licensee concerned.

Part VI - Offences

Unlicensed offshore banking

51.(1) A person who does offshore banking from within Nevis during any period in which he does not hold a licence under this Ordinance is guilty of an offence and liable on conviction to a fine not exceeding two hundred and fifty thousand dollars.

(2) Any director or officer of a company that does offshore banking from within Nevis without a licence under this Ordinance is guilty of an offence and liable on conviction to a fine not exceeding fifty thousand dollars or to imprisonment for five years or to both such fine and imprisonment.

(3) Subject to subsection 4 a person who holds any funds obtained from doing offshore banking business from within Nevis during any period in which he did not hold a licence under this Ordinance shall repay those funds in accordance with the direction of the Minister.

(4) The High Court may order any profits derived from the conduct of offshore banking from within Nevis without a licence under this Ordinance to be forfeited to the Nevis Island Administration.

Misleading advertising

52.(1) A licensee that engages in advertising practices that are likely to mislead concerning

> *(a)* the relationship of the licensee with the Nevis Island Administration or any department or office thereof;

> *(b)* the true interest rate paid on deposit or charged or credit;

> *(c)* the true returns on the management of investments;

(d) the insured or guaranteed status of deposit or other liabilities or of investments managed by it; or

(e) the financial condition of the designated institution; is guilty of an offence and liable on conviction to a fine not exceeding ten thousand dollars.

(2) A licensee shall, in respect of its business, furnish the Permanent Secretary with copies of all its advertisements.

False statement and obstruction

53. A director, officer, employee or agent of a licensee, who, with intent to deceive,

(a) makes any false or misleading statement or entry in a book, account, record, report or statement of the licensee or omits a statement or entry that should be made therein, or

(b) obstructs

(i) the carrying out by an auditor of his proper function under this Ordinance, or

(ii) the examination of a licensee as required pursuant to this Ordinance is guilty of an offence and liable on summary conviction to a fine not exceeding fifty thousand dollars or imprisonment for five years or to both.

Disclosure of confidential information

54. A person referred to in section 39(1) who discloses confidential information contrary to that section is guilty of an offence and liable on conviction to a fine not exceeding twenty thousand dollars or to imprisonment for twelve months or both.

Contravention of section 42

55. A licensee that contravenes section 42 is guilty of an offence and liable on conviction to a fine not exceeding twenty thousand dollars and in addition to a further fine of one thousand dollars for each month during which the offence continues after a conviction is obtained.

Part VII - General

Extending time

56. At the request of a licensee, the Minister may extend the time within which any document or information required from the licensee under this Ordinance must be sent to the Permanent Secretary.

Regulations

57. The Minister may make such regulations as are necessary for the purpose of this Ordinance and, in particular, may make regulations in respect of such acts, matters or things as are required by this Ordinance to be prescribed.

Use of "bank" in names

58.(1) Subject to subsection (2) no person other than a licensee may, without the approval of the Minister use the word

(a)"**bank**" or any of its derivatives in any language, or

(b) any other word indicating the doing of offshore banking from within Nevis, in the name, description or title under which that person carries on business or intends to carry on business in Nevis or make any representation to that effect in any bill head, letter paper, notice or advertisement.

(2) Subsection (1) does not apply

(a) to a bank licensed under the Banking Act;

(b) to a qualified foreign bank or eligible company that is applying for a licence under this Ordinance as a licensee;

(3) A person who contravenes subsection (1) is guilty of an offence and liable on conviction to a fine not exceeding twenty thousand dollars.

Part VIII - Winding-up

Voluntary winding-up

59.(1) Except with the prior written approval of the Minister no licensee may be wound-up voluntarily.

(2) Approval for a voluntary winding-up of a licensee may be given by the Minister only if he is satisfied that

(a) the licensee is solvent and has sufficient assets to repay it depositors and other creditors without delay; and

(b) subject to subsection (3), the winding-up has been approved by the holders of at least two-thirds of the outstanding voting shares of the licensee.

(3) Where the Minister finds in respect of a licensee that there is imminent danger of its insolvency, the Minister may waive the requirement for shareholder approval of the winding-up of the licensee voluntarily, if

(a) the winding-up is to be effected in whole or in part through the sale of any of the assets of the licensee to another licensee; and

(b) the deposit liabilities of the licensee to be wound-up are to be assumed by that other licensee.

Commencement of voluntary winding-up

60. When a licensee receives the approval of the Minister to its voluntary winding-up, the licensee shall

(a) cease to do business immediately and retain only such staff as is necessary for an orderly winding-up;

(b) repay its depositors and other creditors; and

(c) wind-up all operations undertaken before the receipt of the approval to wind-up.

Notice of winding-up

61.(1) Within thirty days of the receipt of the approval of the Minister to the winding-up a notice of voluntary winding-up which must contain the prescribed information, shall be sent by the licensee in the prescribed manner or by personal service, to the depositors and creditors of the licensee and other persons having any interest in its funds or other property.

(2) The notice described in subsection (1) shall also be published in the Gazette and placed in a conspicuous place on the premises of each office or branch of the licensee to be wound-up.

Settlement of claims

62.(1) The approval of the Minister to the voluntary winding-up of a licensee does not adversely affect the rights of a depositor or other creditor of the licensee to settlement in full of his claim nor the rights of any person having an interest in the funds or property of the licensee to settlement of that interest.

(2) All claims made by persons described in subsection (1) shall be settled by the licensee concerned within such time as the Minister may determine.

Distribution of remaining assets

63.(1) The assets of a licensee being voluntarily wound-up that remain after settlement of the claims described in section 62 are to be distributed among the shareholders of the licensee in proportion to their respective rights.

(2) Notwithstanding subsection (1), no distribution of the remaining assets of a licensee may be made

(a) before all claims of depositors and other creditors have been settled or, in the case of a disputed claim, before the licensee has deposited with the Nevis Island Administration sufficient funds to meet any liability that could arise under that claim;

(b) before any funds that are payable to a depositor or other creditor who has made his claim have been deposited with the Nevis Island Administration; or

(c) before any funds or property held by the licensee that could not be returned, in accordance with section 62, to the persons who have an interest therein have been deposited with or transferred to the Nevis Island Administration, together with the relevant records.

Interruption of winding-up

64.(1) If the Minister determines that the assets of a licensee that is being voluntarily wound-up are not sufficient for the full discharge of the obligations of the licensee or that the completion of such a winding-up is being unduly delayed, the Minister may seize the management and control of the licensee by posting a notice to that effect on the premises of the licensee and by putting persons appointed by the Minister into the offices of the licensee.

(2) When the Minister seizes the management and control of a licensee under subsection (1) he shall immediately begin proceedings for the compulsory winding-up of the licensee or its re-organisation, in accordance with this Ordinance.

Seizure in other cases

65.(1) Notwithstanding section 64, the Minister may seize the management and control of a licensee in any of the following circumstances, namely

> *(a)* when the realizable value of the licensee's assets is less than the aggregate of its liabilities and capital accounts or the licensee's financial condition suggests that it will shortly be in that circumstance;

> *(b)* when its business is being conducted in an imprudent manner or is not being conducted in accordance with this Ordinance;

> *(c)* when the licensee refuses to submit to inspection of its records or operations by an auditor appointed under section 44 or an examiner appointed under section 46; or

> *(d)* when its licence has been revoked or suspended under this Ordinance.

(2) A seizure of the management and control of a licensee under this section is effected by placing a notice to that effect on the premises of the licensee and by putting persons appointed by the Minister into the offices of the licensee.

(3) A licensee aggrieved by a seizure under this section may institute proceedings in the High Court for recovery of the administration and control of the institution and the High Court may make such order in respect thereto as to it seems just and consistent with the purposes of this Ordinance.

Duty of Minister

66. Within thirty days after the Minister has seized the administration and control of a licensee under this Ordinance, the Minister shall begin proceedings in the High Court

(a) for the compulsory winding-up of the licensee; or

(b) for the reorganisation of the licensee.

Power of High Court

67. The High Court may in respect of proceedings by the Minister under section 66 order

(a) the compulsory winding-up of the licensee;

(b) the reorganisation of the licensee subject to such terms and conditions as the court may determine; or

(c) the return of the management and control of the licensee to its shareholders, directors and officers subject to such safeguards or conditions, if any, as the court may consider for the purposes of this Ordinance.

Notice of application

68.(1) Forthwith after he makes an application to the High Court under section 66 in relation to a licensee, the Minister shall give notice of the application

(a) to the directors and shareholders of the licensee, and

(b) to the depositors and other creditors of the licensee.

Appointment of custodian

69. If the High Court orders the compulsory winding-up or reorganisation of a licensee pursuant to an application under section 67, the High Court shall appoint a custodian to be responsible to the Court and to supervise the winding-up or re-organisation of the licensee.

Functions of custodian

70.(1) In respect of the licensee for which he has been appointed, the custodian has the exclusive power and duty to manage and control the affairs of the licensee.

(2) Without limiting his powers or duties under subsection (1) , the custodian may, in respect of the licensee for which he has been appointed,

(a) continue or discontinue its operations;

(b) stop or limit the payment of its obligations;

(c) employ staff;

(d) execute any instrument in its name;

(e) initiate, defend and conduct in its name any action or proceeding to which the licensee is or might be a party;

(f) end the seizure of the licensee by restoring it to its directors and shareholders; and

(g) re-organise or wind-up the licensee in accordance with this Ordinance.

Inventory of assets

71.(1) Forthwith after assuming management and control of a licensee, the custodian shall make an inventory of its assets and forward a copy of the inventory to the Registrar of the High Court.

(2) The copy of the inventory forwarded to the Registrar shall be kept available at all reasonable times for the inspection of interested persons.

Reorganisation

72.(1) Where the re-organisation of a licensee has been ordered by the High Court, the custodian shall develop a plan of re-organisation and deliver a copy thereof to each of the depositors and other creditors of the licensee who under the plan would not receive full restitution or payment of their claims.

(2) The copy of the re-organisation plan must be accompanied by a notice requiring that objections to the plan be delivered to the custodian not later than thirty days after the last of the copies have been delivered under subsection (1).

(3) If within the time limited therefor by subsection (2) the custodian does not receive objections in writing to the re-organisation from persons who in the aggregate hold at least one-third of the total amount of deposits and other liabilities of the licensee, the custodian may carry out the re-organisation plan referred to in subsection (1).

(4) When an objection to the re-organisation plan is received from one-third or more of the persons described in subsection (3), the custodian shall submit further re-organisation plans in like manner until such time as fewer than one-third of the persons described in subsection (3) object within the time limited therefor or he may refer the matter back, at anytime to the High Court for further directions.

(5) The High Court may extend the time limited by subsection (1) and upon cause shown may exempt the custodian from delivering the plan to some or all of the persons mentioned in subsection (1).

Content of plan

73. A re-organisation plan developed by the custodian of a licensee must, so far as it is practicable to do so

(a) be equitable to all classes of depositors;

(b) provide for bringing in new funds to establish adequate ratios between

(i) capital and deposits, and

(ii) liquid assets and deposits; and

*(c)*provide for the removal of any directors or any officer or employee responsible for the circumstances that led to the seizure of the licensee.

Application for order by custodian

74. If, in the course of the re-organisation of a licensee, it appears to the custodian that circumstances render the plan or its execution undesirable, he may apply to the High Court for an order

(a) to modify the plan, or

(b) to wind-up the licensee compulsorily.

Compulsory winding-up

75.(1) Where the High Court under section 67 or 74 orders the compulsory winding-up of a licensee, the custodian appointed therefor by the Court may, subject to subsection (2), perform the functions of the licensee.

(2) The custodian of a licensee described in subsection (1) may not, without an order of the High Court to do so,

(a) sell any assets or transfer any property of the licensee that has a value exceeding one hundred thousand dollars;

(b) create a security interest in any asset or property of the licensee in favour of a creditor who extends a new credit to the licensee;

(c) compromise or release any claim the amount of which exceeds one hundred thousand dollars; or

(d) pay any claim other than one in respect of an obligation incurred by the custodian in the exercise of his winding-up functions before the schedule referred to in section 79(c) has been approved by the High Court.

Termination of service contracts

76. Subject to any other law governing conditions of employment, the custodian of a licensee that has been ordered by the High Court to be compulsorily wound-up shall terminate not later than nine months after the order of the High Court

(a) any employment contract of the licensee;

(b) any contract for services which the licensee is a party, and

(c) any obligations of the licensee as a lessee of property.

Right of lessor

77. A lessor of any property referred to in section 76

(a) must be given notice of not less than ninety days of the intended termination of the obligations of a licensee thereunder;

(b) has no claim for rent thereunder other than rent accrued on the date of the termination of the obligation of the licensee; and

(c) has no right to damages by reason only of any termination of the obligations of the licensee, notwithstanding any term of the lease to the contrary.

Statements of accounts

78.(1) Within sixty days after an order for the compulsory winding-up of a licensee, the custodian shall deliver a statement of account to any depositors and other creditors.

(2) The statement of account is a statement of the nature and amount for which a claim of a person described in subsection (1) is shown on the books of the licensee.

(3) A notice specifying that any objection to the statement of account is to be made on a date specified in the notice, not being later than sixty days after the delivery of the notice, must accompany the statement of account.

(4) The High Court on application of the custodian for cause shown may exempt the custodian from delivering a statement of account to any person mentioned in subsection (1).

Claims

79. Not later than ninety days after the last day specified in the notice for filing claims against a licensee being compulsorily wound-up, the custodian shall

(a) reject any claim, of which he doubts the validity;

(b) determine the amount, if any, owing to each known depositor or other creditor and the priority of his claim under this Ordinance;

(c) prepare for filing with the High Court a schedule of the actions proposed to be undertaken for the purpose of the compulsory winding-up of the licensee;

(d) notify each person whose claim is allowed in full; and

(e) publish, once a week for three consecutive weeks in a newspaper of general circulation in Nevis,

(i) a notice of the date and place where the schedule referred to in paragraph (c) will be available for inspection, and

(ii) the date, not being earlier than thirty days from the date of the publication, on which the custodian will file that schedule with the High Court.

Objections

80.(1) Within twenty days of the filing of a schedule under section 79, a depositor or other creditor or shareholder of the licensee concerned, or other interested person, may file with the High Court any objection he has to any action proposed in the schedule referred to in section 79(c).

(2) After notice served on the custodian and such interested parties as the High Court may require, the High Court shall hear the objection and make such order thereon as it considers just in the circumstances.

(3) When the High Court allows an objection, the order must set out the manner in which the schedule referred to in section 79(c) is to be modified.

Distribution of assets

81.(1) When a schedule has been filed under section 79 in respect of a licensee, the custodian may make a partial distribution to the claimants against the licensee whose claims are undisputed or allowed by the High Court, if the custodian establishes an adequate reserve for the payment of disputed claims against the licensee.

(2) As soon as practicable after all objections against the distribution proposed by the custodian have been heard and determined, final distribution of the assets of the licensee concerned shall be made by the custodian.

Priority of claims

82.(1) The following claims have priority against the general assets of a licensee being compulsorily wound-up under this Ordinance

(a) firstly, the necessary and reasonable expenses incurred by the custodian in carrying out his functions under this Ordinance;

(b) secondly, the wages and salaries of the officers and employees of the licensee that accrued during the three months immediately preceding the seizure of the licensee under this Ordinance;

(c) thirdly, any monies owing to the Nevis Island Administration;

(d) fourthly, the other deposits.

(2) After payment of all other claims against the licensee, with interest at such rate as the High Court determines, all remaining claims against the licensee that were not filed within the time limited therefor under this Ordinance may then be paid.

(3) Where the amount available to pay the claims of any class of claimant specified in this section in respect of priorities is not sufficient to provide payment in full to claimants in that class, the amount available shall be distributed by the custodian on a pro rata basis among the claimants in that class.

Distribution to shareholders

83. The assets of a licensee being compulsorily wound-up that remain after the final distribution to claimants pursuant to section 82 shall be distributed by the custodian among the shareholders of the licensee in proportion to their respective rights.

Abandoned funds

84.(1) Any funds of a licensee being compulsorily wound-up under this Ordinance that remain unclaimed after the final distribution under section 82 and not subject to distribution under any other provision of this Ordinance shall be deposited with the Nevis Island Administration by the custodian of the licensee.

(2) Funds deposited with it under subsection (1) must be held by the Nevis Island Administration for ten years unless earlier claimed by a person entitled thereto.

(3) On the expiration of the ten years referred to in subsection (1) in respect of any funds, those funds remaining unclaimed become abandoned property.

Completion of winding-up

85.(1) When all the assets of a licensee being wound-up have been distributed or dealt with as required by this Ordinance, the custodian shall render an audited statement to the High Court.

(2) If the High Court is satisfied with the audited statement rendered by the custodian in respect of a licensee being wound-up, it may by order direct the Registrar of the companies to strike the name of the licensee from the register of companies under the Companies Act and publish notice thereof in the Gazette.

(3) When its name is struck off the register of companies the licensee is thereupon dissolved and its licence under this Ordinance is revoked.

Part IX - Residence

Residents of Nevis

86.(1) For the purposes of this Ordinance, the following are residents of Nevis, namely:

> *(a)* an individual ordinarily resident in Nevis or a citizen of St. Kitts and Nevis with a residence in Nevis;

> *(b)* any incorporated or other body, incorporated, formed or organised in Nevis the majority of the shares or other ownership of which is not beneficially held by persons resident outside Nevis;

> *(c)* any incorporated or other body, wherever incorporated, formed or organised, that is controlled within the meaning of section 22 by a person described in paragraph (a) or (b);

> *(d)* any incorporated body or other body that is controlled within the meaning of section 22 by a body described in paragraph (c) or by the Nevis Island Administration or any agency thereof;

(2) A reference in this Part to any beneficial interest, or to any thing being beneficially owned or held includes ownership through a trustee, legal representative, agent or other intermediary.

Persons resident outside Nevis

87. A person is resident outside Nevis for the purpose of this Ordinance if he is not a resident of Nevis within the meaning of section 86.

Part X - Tax Exemptions

Exemption from tax

88.(1) Except as provided by this Part, no income tax, capital gains tax or other direct tax shall be levied in Nevis upon the profits or gains of a licensee in respect of the offshore banking it does from within Nevis.

(2) Except as provided by this Part, no income tax, capital gains tax or other direct tax shall be levied in Nevis in respect of any dividends or earnings attributable to the shares or securities of a licensee that are beneficially owned by another licensee or by a person who is not a resident of Nevis.

(3) Except as provided by this Part, no estate, inheritance, succession or similar tax shall be levied in Nevis in respect of any shares, securities or assets of a licensee that are beneficially owned by a person who is not a resident of Nevis.

(4) Except as provided by this Part, no tax or duty shall be levied upon the increment in value of the property or other assets in Nevis of a licensee other than upon such of them as are distributed to residents of Nevis.

Transfer of assets exemption

89.(1) Except as provided by this Part, no tax or duty shall be levied upon a licensee, its shareholders or transferees in respect of the transfer of all or any part of its securities or other assets to another licensee or to a person who is not a resident of Nevis.

(2) Where a person who is not a resident of Nevis or a licensee transfers shares of a licensee that are held by that person or licensee to another person who is not a resident of Nevis or to another licensee, the transfer is exempt from the payment of any tax or duty thereon.

(3) Except as provided by this Part,

    (a) no income tax or capital gains tax, and

    (b) no other direct tax shall be levied or collected in Nevis in respect of any dividend, interest or other return from any shares, securities, deposits or other borrowing of a licensee or any assets managed by the licensee if the dividend, interest or other returns are in respect of shares, securities deposits or other borrowings or assets beneficially owned by a person who is not a resident of Nevis; but the onus of establishing ownership lies upon the licensee

Withholding tax and report re dividends etc.

90.(1) Notwithstanding any provision of the Income Tax Act, but subject to subsection (2), no licensee need withhold any portion of any dividend, interest or other returns payable to any person in respect of any borrowings of the licensee or in respect of that person holding shares or securities of the licensee.

(2) All dividends, interest or other returns attributable to the shares or securities of or the management of assets by a licensee that are payable to a resident of Nevis and known as such by the licensee shall be reported to the Inland Revenue Department.

Tax on profits

91.(1) By way of income tax but in lieu of income tax at the rates in the Income Tax Act, there shall be levied and paid to the Inland Revenue Department upon the profits and gains of a licensee, in respect of the offshore banking business done by it from within Nevis, tax at the following rates *(a)* 2½% on all profits and gains up to ten million dollars;

(b) 2% on all profits and gains in amounts exceeding ten million dollars but not exceeding twenty million dollars;

(c) 1½% on all profits and gains in amounts exceeding twenty million dollars but not exceeding thirty million dollars; and

(d) 1% on all profits and gains in amounts exceeding thirty million dollars.

(2) Except in so far as this Ordinance operates to exempt a licensee from liability to income tax under the Income Tax Act, the provisions of that Act apply *mutatis mutandis* to a licensee.

Tax agreement

92.(1) Notwithstanding section 91, a licensee and the Minister may enter into an agreement determining the amount to be paid as income tax in lieu of other taxes on income by the licensee in respect of the business it does from within Nevis.

(2) An agreement under subsection (1) may not provide for any amount in lieu of other taxes if it would result in the licensee paying less than it would if it were to pay tax pursuant to section 91.

Service Fees etc.

93.(1) When a tax levied in Nevis is in the nature of a service charge or utility charge for a service provided by the Nevis Island Administration, a licensee is not exempt from that charge under this Part.

(2) A service or utility charge includes a charge or fee levied or imposed for the issuance of any incorporation, registration or licence required in Nevis.

Customs duty

94. The Minister may by order exempt a licensee in respect of its business from all or so much of any duty payable under the Customs Act in respect of any goods imported by the licensee in respect of its business as the Minister deems expedient, if the licensee in respect of its business satisfies the Minister that the goods concerned are not being made or manufactured in Nevis, are essential as equipment or fixtures for doing business from within Nevis and are not merely goods that will be used up or expended in the ordinary course of business.

Employee benefits

95.(1) Where the Minister is satisfied that a licensee must use the services of specially qualified persons in order to do its business effectively from within Nevis and that

(a) it is unable to acquire those services in Nevis, and

(b) it is unable to retain or hire those services from outside Nevis without special tax benefits being made available the Minister may authorise an offshore benefit provision for the employment of those specially qualified persons.

(2) An offshore benefit provisions is one whereby a prescribed percentage of an employee's or contractor's salary or fees from a licensee

(a) is exempt from any duty or tax in Nevis;

(b) may be paid in a foreign currency;

(c) may be paid in some other prescribed manner in another currency or otherwise; notwithstanding the provision of any other law to the contrary.

Part XI - Miscellaneous and Consequential

Application of Companies Act

96.(1) The provisions of the Companies Act relating to the winding-up of a company do not apply to a licensee.

Bankruptcy Act

97 . The Bankruptcy Act does not apply to a licensee.

Banking Act

98. The Banking Act does not apply to a licensee in respect of its offshore banking business.

Exemptions

99. The provisions of this Ordinance set out hereunder do not apply to a licensee that is a qualified foreign bank, namely:

> *(a)* sections 20 to 24;

> *(b)* sections 33 to 37;

> *(c)* Part VIII.

Commencement

100. This Ordinance comes into operation on a day to be fixed by the Minister.

Part 7 - Registration Of International Trusts

Registration of trusts

37.(1) The registrar shall maintain a register of international trusts.

(2) An application for entry on the register shall be accompanied by -

(a) the prescribed fee;

(b) notice of the name and registered office of the trust;

(c) a certificate from a trustee company, a barrister or solicitor certifying that the trust upon registration will be an international trust.

(3) The Registrar shall, on receipt of the prescribed fee, the notice and certificate required under sub-section (2) -

(a) enter on the register the name of the trust, and the address of the registered office of the trust;

(b) issue a certificate of registration in the prescribed form.

(4) A certificate of registration under the hand and seal of the registrar shall be conclusive evidence that all the requirements of this Ordinance in respect of registration have been complied with.

Annual certificate of registration

38.(1) A Certificate of registration issued in accordance with sub-section (4) of the preceding section shall be valid and effective for a period of one year from the date of registration specified in that certificate.

(2) An application for renewal of registration shall be made by -

(a) filing with the Registrar an application for renewal in the prescribed form; and

(b) payment of the prescribed fee.

(3) An application for renewal of registration may be made before the date of expiry of the last certificate of registration and no application for renewal of registration shall be granted unless such application is in accordance with sub-section (2) hereof.

(4) Every renewal of registration shall take effect from the date of expiry of the last certificate of registration.

(5) Every renewal of registration shall be for a period of one year from the date of expiry of the last certificate of registration.

Notification of termination

39. Where an international trust which has been registered terminates, the trustee shall notify the Registrar and return the certificate of registration and the Registrar shall then cancel the entry on the register and cancel the certificate of registration.

Inspection of register

40. The register shall not be open for inspection except that a trustee of a trust may in writing authorise a person to inspect the entry of that trust on the register.

Minister may increase fees

41. The Minister may increase the fees payable by Order published in the Gazette.

Registered office

42.(1) The registered office of an international trust shall be the office of the trust company or corporation which is a trustee.

(2) The address for service of any documents upon an international trust shall be the registered office of that trust.

Part 8 - Exemption From Taxes

Exemption from taxes and duties

43. Notwithstanding any provision to the contrary in any enactment, a trust registered under this Ordinance shall be exempt from -

(a) all income tax;

(b) all estate, inheritance, succession and gift tax payable with respect to the trust property by reason of any death;

(c) stamp duty with respect to all instruments relating to the trust property or to transactions carried out by the trustee on behalf of the trust;

(d) all exchange controls.

Part 9 - Miscellaneous

Commencement of proceedings

44.(1) No action or proceeding whether pursuant to this Ordinance or at common law or in equity -

> *(a)* to set aside the settlement of an international trust;

> *(b)* to set aside any disposition to any international trust; or

> *(c)* against a trustee or trustees for breach of trust shall be commenced, unless such action or proceeding is commenced in the High Court of St. Christopher and Nevis before the expiration of 2 years from -

> *(d)* the date of the settlement of the international trust that is sought to be set aside;

> *(e)* the disposition to the international trust that is sought to be set aside; or

> *(f)* the breach of trust by the trustee or trustees; as the case may be.

(2) No action or proceeding whether pursuant to this Ordinance or at common law or in equity shall be commenced by any person; -

> *(a)* claiming to have had an interest in property before that property was settled upon or disposed to an international trust; and

> *(b)* seeking to derive a legal or equitable interest in that property; unless such action or proceeding is commenced in the High Court of St. Christopher and Nevis before the expiration of 2 years

from the date that the property referred to in paragraphs (a) and (b) was settled upon or disposed to an international trust.

(3) No action or proceeding to which sub-sections (1) or (2) of this section or to which section 24 shall apply, whether substantive or interlocutory in nature, shall be determined and no order shall be made, or granted by the Court (including any injunction that shall have the effect of preventing the exercise of, or restoring to a person any rights, duties, obligations or power or preserving, granting custody of, detaining or inspecting any property) unless, the applicant shall first satisfy the Court by affidavit, that -

(a) the action or proceeding has been commenced in accordance with sub-sections (1) or (2) of this section;

(b) where the action or proceeding shall allege fraud or be founded upon some other action or proceeding alleging fraud, the determination or order sought would not be contrary to the provisions of section 24;

(c) that the requirements of section 55 have been fulfilled.

(4) Every affidavit required to be filed pursuant to sub-section (3) shall be made by the person on whose behalf the action or proceeding is brought or, in the case of a body corporate, an officer thereof, and every such person or officer as the case may be, shall depose as to, -

(a) the circumstances of the cause of action in respect of which the action or proceedings are brought;

(b) the date upon which the cause of action shall have accrued;

(c) the date upon which the property, in respect of which the action or proceeding is brought, was settled on or disposed to the international trust;

(d) whether an action or proceeding have been commenced in respect of the cause of action and if so, the date upon which that action or those proceedings were commenced.

(5) The provisions of this section shall apply to every international trust expressed to be governed by the law of Nevis and, in the event that a trust shall be registered as an international trust, and shall change the law by which it shall be governed to that of Nevis, then every proceeding after the date of registration by a person claiming to interested in, or to be prejudiced by, the settlement or property upon such trust, or any disposition of property to such trust before registration, shall be commenced subject to sub-sections (1) and (2) and every determination and order shall be made subject to sub-section (3) as if upon the date that such settlement or disposition was made the trust was an international trust governed by the law of the Nevis.

Investments

45.(1) A trustee shall not invest any of the trust funds other than in securities, assets, or property authorised expressly or by necessary implication for the investment of the trust funds by and under the instrument by which the trust is established or created.

(2) Where the instrument by which the trust is created or established authorises expressly or by necessary implication the investment of the trust funds in any investments authorised by the laws of St. Christopher and Nevis for the investment of trust funds the instrument shall be deemed to authorise investment as expressed in the Schedule to this Ordinance.

Bankruptcy

46. Notwithstanding any provision of the law of the settlor's domicile or place of ordinary residence of the settlor's current place of incorporation and notwithstanding further that an international trust is voluntary and without valuable consideration being given for the same or is made for the benefit of the settlor's spouse or children, an international trust shall not be void or voidable in the event of the settlor's bankruptcy, insolvency of liquidation (other than in the case of an international company registered pursuant to the Nevis Business Corporation Ordinance 1984, that is in liquidation) or in any action or proceeding at the suit of creditors of the settlor, but shall remain valid and subsisting and take effect according to its tenor subject to sections 23 and 24 of this Ordinance.

Retention of control by settlor

47. An international trust shall not be declared invalid or be affected in any way if the settlor, and if more than one, any of them either -

(a) retains, possesses or acquires power to revoke the trust;

(b) retains, possesses or acquires power to amend the trust;

(c) retains, possesses or acquires any benefit, interest or property from the trust;

(d) retains, possesses or acquires the power to remove or appoint a trustee or protector;

(e) retains, possesses or acquires the power to direct a trustee or protector on any matter;

(f) is the beneficiary of the trust solely or together with others.

Heirship rights

48. No international trust or any aspect of such trust governed by this Ordinance and no disposition of property to be held upon the trusts thereof shall be declared void, voidable or defective in any manner nor is the capacity of any settlor to be questioned by reason that such trust may avoid or defeat the right, claim or interest of a person held by reason of a personal relationship to the settlor or by way of heirship rights.

Statute of Elizabeth

49. The enactment titled 13 Elizabeth 1 Ch 5 (1571) shall have no application to any international trust that is governed by this Ordinance nor any provision thereof nor to any transfer into such trust.

Translations

50.(1) Every document filed with the Registrar and not in English shall be accompanied by a certified translation.

(2) A document not in the English language and not accompanied by a certified translation at the time of filing shall not be accepted for registration by the Registrar.

(3) For the purpose of this section a certified translation is a translation in the English language, certified as a correct translation, be a translator to the satisfaction of the Registrar.

Immunity from suit

51. No action shall be against the Nevis Island Administration, any statutory body or authority or a public or judicial officer in respect of any act or failure to act in accordance with the provisions of this Ordinance.

Prohibition by Minister

52.(1) The Minister may by Order -

(a) prohibit the registration of an international trust;

(b) direct any international trust to cease carrying on its business or any part of its business immediately or within such time as may be specified in the Order.

(2) An order made under this section may be revoked or varied at any time by the Minister.

Definition of trust

53. A trust exists where a person (known as "a trustee") holds or has vested in him, property which does not form, or which has ceased to form part of his own estate

(a) for the benefit of any person (known as "a beneficiary") whether or not yet ascertained or in existence; or

(b) for any valid charitable or non-charitable purpose which is not for the benefit only of the trustee; or

(c) for such benefit as is mentioned in sub-paragraph (a) and also for any such purpose as is mentioned in sub-paragraph (b).

Power to establish advisory bodies

54.(1) The Minister may establish advisory bodies for matters affecting the offshore financial sector in Nevis either by virtue of this Ordinance or the Nevis Business Corporation Ordinance; and each body so established, shall consist of such members as the Minister may from time to time appoint.

(2) In establishing a body under sub-section (1) above, the Minister shall have regard to the desirability of having members who have the expertise and knowledge of the particular area.

(3) It shall be the duty of an advisory body established under this section to advise the Minister on any matter which is referred to it by the Minister

(4) The Minister may defray or contribute towards the expenses of an advisory body established under this section.

Bond

55. Every creditor before bringing any action or proceeding against any trust property governed by this Ordinance shall first deposit with the Permanent Secretary in the Ministry of Finance a bond in the sum of $25,000.00 from a financial institution in Nevis, for securing the payment of all costs as may become payable by the creditor in the event of his not succeeding in such action or proceeding against the trust property.

Community property

56.(1) Where a husband and wife transfer property to an international trust or a trust that subsequently becomes an international trust and, immediately before being transferred, such property or any part of any accumulation thereto is, pursuant to the law of its location or the law either of the transferors' domicile or residence, determined to be community property, then notwithstanding such transfer and except where the provisions of the trust deed may provide to the contrary, that property and any accumulation thereto shall, for the purpose of giving effect to that law, be deemed to be community property and be dealt with in a manner consistent with that law but in every other respect shall be dealt with in accordance with the trust deed and the governing law of that deed.

(2) Notwithstanding anything to the contrary herein contained, nothing herein shall be construed so as to cause the trust, the trust fund, the trustees or any of them, to be liable or obligated for any debt or responsibility of the settlor merely by reason of this section.

Confidentiality, No. 2 of 1985

57.(1) The Confidential Relationships Act shall apply to every trust registered under this Ordinance.

(2) All judicial proceedings, other than criminal proceedings relating to international trusts, shall be heard in camera and no details of the proceedings shall be published by any person without leave of the Court.

Regulations

58.(1) The Minister may make regulations for the better carrying out of the provisions of this Ordinance and for prescribing anything that needs to be prescribed.

(2) The Minister shall prescribe all fees under this Ordinance.

Schedule - Section 45

Authorised Trustee Investments

1. The following shall be regarded as authorised investments:

(a) securities issued by, or the payment of interest on which is guaranteed by, the Nevis Island Administration;

(b) securities issued by, or the payment of interest on which is guaranteed by, any of the following:

(i) the government of the United Kingdom;

(ii) the government of the United States of America;

(iii) the government of any territory within the Commonwealth;

(iv) the African Development Bank, the Asian Development Bank, the Caribbean Development Bank, the European Economic Community, the European Investment Bank, the International Finance Corporation, the International Monetary Fund, or the International Bank for Reconstruction and Development;

(c) deposits with a company registered under the Companies Act (Cap. 335) that is a licensed financial institution within the meaning of the Banking Act No. 6 of 1991;

(d) debentures issued by a quoted company;

(e) quoted shares.

2. In this Schedule, unless the context otherwise requires, the following expressions have the following meanings: -

"**approved stock exchange**" means The International Stock Exchange of the United Kingdom and Republic of Ireland Limited (including the Unlisted Security Market of the International Stock Exchange), the New York Stock Exchange, the American Stock Exchange and the National Association of Security Dealers' Automated Quotation System of the United States of America, the Hang Seng Index, the Nikkei Average or any other stock exchange approved by the Minister;

"**debentures**" includes debenture stock and bonds, whether constituting a charge on assets or not, and loan stock or notes;

"**quoted company**" means a company the ordinary shares in which are quoted on an approved stock exchange;

"**quoted shares**" means shares quoted on an approved stock exchange;

"**securities**" includes shares, debentures, treasury bills and tax reserve certificates;

"shares" include stock.

Nevis Limited Liability Company Ordinance, 1995 - (as amended, 1999)

An Ordinance to provide for the establishment of limited liability companies in the island of Nevis and provide for matters relating thereto or connected therewith.

Be It Enacted by the Queen's Most Excellent Majesty by and with the advice and consent of the Nevis Island Assembly and by the Authority of the same as follows:

Part I - General Provisions

Short Title and commencement

1. This Ordinance may be cited as the Nevis Limited Liability Company Ordinance, 1995 and shall come into operation on the 1st May, 1995.

Interpretation

2. In this Ordinance, unless the context otherwise requires, the term:

"**Articles of organization**" includes

(i) the original articles of organization or any other instrument filed or issued under any law to form a domestic or foreign limited liability company, amended, supplemented, corrected or restated by articles of amendment, merger or consolidation, or other instruments of like effect filed or issued under any law; or

(ii) a special law or charter creating a domestic or foreign limited liability company as amended, supplemented or restated;

"**Business entity**" means a corporation, business trust, estate, trust, partnership, limited liability company, association, joint venture, custodian, nominee, government, governmental subdivision, agency, instrumentality, or any other legal or commercial entity, whether foreign or domestic;

"**Capital contribution**" means any cash, property, services rendered, or a promissory note or other obligation to contribute cash or property or to perform services, which a person contributes to a limited liability company in his capacity as a member;

"**Corporation**" means any incorporated organization or similar entity formed under the laws of any country or jurisdiction;

"**Court**" means a court of law or equity having jurisdiction in any country;

"**Distribution**" means a transfer of money, property or other benefit from a limited liability company to, or for the benefit of a member in his capacity as a member, or to, or for the benefit of, an assignee of a member's interest in the limited liability company, in respect of their limited liability company interest;

"**Foreign limited liability company**" means an entity that is an unincorporated association organised under the laws of any foreign country or other foreign jurisdiction that affords its members, pursuant to the laws under which it is organized, limited liability with respect to the liabilities of the entity;

"**High Court**" means the High Court having jurisdiction in St. Kitts and Nevis;

"**Insolvent**" means being unable to pay debts as they become due in the usual course of the debtor's business;

"**Limited liability company**", "domestic limited liability company" and "company" means a limited liability company formed under this Ordinance;

"**Manager**" means -

> *(a)* a person or persons, whether or not a member, designated and authorized in the operating agreement to manage the limited liability company or to otherwise act as agent of the limited liability

company, either to execute management duties generally or to execute certain management duties as specified in the operating agreement;

(b) where the operating agreement does not designate a person or persons as a manager or managers, or the operating agreement designates as managers all of the members, in their capacity as members, references in this Ordinance to managers shall mean each of the members of the limited liability company, to the extent management duties are assigned to the members in the operating agreement, or if not so assigned, then without limitation;

(c) where the operating agreement designates one or more members as a manager or managers, or one or more manager or managers who are not members of the limited liability company, references in this Ordinance to managers shall mean each of the managers of the limited liability company so designated, to the extent management duties are assigned to each such member in the operating agreement, or if not so assigned, then without limitation;

"**Member**" means a person who has been admitted to a limited liability company as a member pursuant to section 36 of this Ordinance, or, in the case of a foreign limited liability company, in accordance with the laws of the foreign country or foreign jurisdiction under which the foreign limited liability company is organized;

"**Member's interest**" means a member's share of the profits, losses, income, gain, deductions and credits of the limited liability company, the right to receive distributions from the limited liability company and all of the member's rights and obligations under this Ordinance, the articles of organization, and the operating agreement;

"**Minister of Finance**" means the Minister for the time being charged with the responsibility of Finance in the Nevis Island Administration;

"**Operating agreement**" means the agreement, and any amendments thereto, of the members as to the affairs of a limited liability company, the conduct of its business, and the relations among the members;

"**Organize**r" means a person who forms a limited liability company pursuant to section 21;

"**Person**" means an individual or a business entity;

"**Registrar of Companies**" means the person appointed by the Minister to perform the duties of Registrar under this Ordinance;

"**Termination of a member's interest**" means a complete cessation of a member's continued membership in a limited liability company for any reason;

"**Transfer**" means the sale, assignment, mortgage, creation or permission to subsist of any pledge, lien, charge or encumbrance over, conveyance, lease, gift, grant of any interest or other rights in or other disposition of any member's interest, any part thereof or any interest therein, whether by agreement, operation of law or otherwise.

Application of this Ordinance

3. Any limited liability company formed or subject to this Ordinance which does business in Nevis shall be subject to and comply with all requirements of the Companies Act (Cap. 335) in the same manner as a company formed thereunder.

Form of instruments; filing

4.(1) Whenever any provision of this Ordinance requires any instrument to be filed with the Registrar of Companies, such instrument shall comply with the provisions of this Part unless otherwise expressly provided by law.

(2) Every instrument referenced herein, filed or required to be filed, shall be in the English language, except that the corporate name may be in another language if written in English letters or characters.

(3) All instruments shall be signed by at least one manager duly authorized by the limited liability company to sign such instruments on behalf of the company, or such other person duly delegated such authority by the manager or managers in whom such authority resides.

(4) Whenever any provision of this Ordinance requires an instrument to be acknowledged, such requirement means in the case of execution of an instrument within Nevis that:

(a) the person signing the instrument shall acknowledge that it is his act and deed or that it is the act and deed of the limited liability company, as the case may be; and

(b) the instrument shall be acknowledged before a notary public, commissioner for oaths or other person authorized to take acknowledgments, who shall attest that he knows the person making the acknowledgment to be the person who executed the instrument.

(5) In the case of the execution of an instrument outside of Nevis, an acknowledgment shall mean;

(a) the person signing the instrument shall acknowledge that it is his act and deed or that it is the act and deed of the limited liability company, as the case may be; and

(b) the instrument shall be acknowledged before a notary public or any other person authorized to take acknowledgments according to the laws of the place of execution, or a consul or vice-consul of St. Christopher and Nevis or other governmental official of St. Christopher and Nevis authorized to take acknowledgments or, in their absence, a consular official of another government having diplomatic relations with St. Christopher and Nevis, and such notary, person, consul or vice-consul shall attest that he knows the person making the acknowledgment to be the person who executed the instrument; and

(c) when the acknowledgment shall be taken by a notary public or any other person authorized to take acknowledgments, except a governmental official of St. Christopher or Nevis or foreign consular official, the signature of such person who has authority shall be attested to by a consul or vice-consul of the Federation of St. Christopher and Nevis or, in his absence, by a consular official of another government having diplomatic relation with St. Christopher and Nevis or a government official of the place of execution who is authorized to make such attestation, or an Apostille according to the Convention de la Haye 5 Octobre 1961.

(6) Whenever any provision of this Ordinance requires any instrument to be filed with the Registrar of Companies, such requirement means that:

(a) an appropriate receipt evidencing payment of all appropriate fees shall be delivered to the office of the Registrar of Companies

and, within ten days of the date of the receipt, the original instrument together with a duplicate instrument, both signed and acknowledged;

(b) upon delivery of the original signed and acknowledged instrument with the required receipt and an exact signed and acknowledged copy the Registrar of Companies shall certify that the instrument has been filed in his office by endorsing the word "Filed" and the date of the required receipt upon the original instrument. Said date shall be the filing date;

(c) the Registrar of Companies shall compare the duplicate signed and acknowledged copy with the original signed and acknowledged instrument, and if he finds that the text is identical shall affix on the duplicate copy the same endorsement of filing as he affixed on the original. The said original, as endorsed shall be returned to the limited liability company. The endorsement constitutes the certificate of the Registrar of Companies that the document is a true copy of the instrument filed in his office and that it was filed as of the date stated in the endorsement; and

(d) any instrument filed in accordance with this subsection shall be effective as of the filing date stated thereon.

(7) Any instrument relating to a domestic or foreign limited liability company and filed with the Registrar of Companies under this Ordinance may be corrected with respect to any error apparent on the face or defect in the execution thereof by filing with the Registrar of Companies a certificate of correction, executed and acknowledged in the manner required for the original instrument. The certificate of correction shall specify the error or defect to be corrected and shall set forth the portion of the instrument in correct form. The corrected instrument when filed shall be effective as of the date the original instrument was filed.

Certificates or certified copies as evidence

5. All certificates issued by the Registrar of Companies in accordance with the provisions of this Ordinance and all copies of documents filed in his office in accordance with the provisions of this Ordinance shall, when certified by him, be taken and received in all courts, public offices and official bodies as *prima facie* evidence of the facts therein stated and of the execution of such instruments.

Fees on filing articles of organization and other documents

6. (1*)* The Minister of Finance is hereby empowered to promulgate and shall so promulgate a schedule of fees for the filing and issuance of documents under this Ordinance. Fees payable in respect of this Ordinance shall be payable in Eastern Caribbean dollars, or upon the authorization of the Minister of Finance, in any other currency.

(2) Fees for certifying copies of documents and for filing, recording or indexing papers shall be fixed by the Minister of Finance.

Annual registration Fee

7. Every limited liability company shall pay to the Minister of Finance an annual fee as prescribed in the schedule required to be promulgated by the Minister of Finance under this Ordinance.

Waiver of notice

8. Whenever any notice is required to be given to any member or manager of a limited liability company or to any other person under the provisions of this Ordinance or the operating agreement of the limited liability company, a waiver thereof in writing, signed by the person or persons entitled to such notice, whether before or after the time stated therein, shall be deemed to be equivalent to the giving of such notice.

Notice to members

9. Any notice or information required to be given to members shall be provided in the manner designated in the limited liability company's operating agreement or, if the notice can no longer be provided as stated therein, the notice shall be published in a publication of general circulation in Nevis or in a place where the limited liability company has a place of business. Any notice requiring a shareholder to take action in order to secure a right or privilege shall be published or given in time to allow a reasonable opportunity for such action to be taken.

Information and records

10.(1) Each member of a limited liability company has the right, at his own expense and subject to such reasonable standards (including standards governing what information and documents are to be furnished) as may be set forth in the operating agreement or otherwise established by the managers, to obtain from the limited liability company from time to time upon reasonable demand for any purpose reasonably related to the member's interest as a member of the limited liability company such information and records as the limited liability company may maintain.

(2) Each manager shall have the right to examine all of the information described in subsection (1) for a purpose reasonably related to his position as a manager.

(3) The manager of a limited liability company shall have the right to keep confidential from the members, for such period of time as the manager deems reasonable, any information which the manager reasonably believes to be in the nature of trade secrets or other information the disclosure of which the manager in good faith believes is not in the best interest of the limited liability company or could damage the limited liability company or its business or which the limited liability company is required by law or by agreement with a third party to keep confidential.

(4) Any demand by a member under this section shall be in writing and shall state the purpose of such demand.

(5) Any action to enforce any right arising under this section shall be brought in the High Court.

(6) Failure of the limited liability company to keep or maintain records shall not be grounds for imposing liability on any manager, officer, member or agent of the limited liability company for debts, obligations and liabilities of the limited liability company.

Construction

11. In construing this Ordinance, or any part hereof, the Courts or any other person shall refer to the common law or to the construction of the same or similar Acts in other jurisdictions.

Part II - Purposes And Powers

Purposes

12. Limited liability companies may be organized under this Ordinance for any lawful business purpose or purposes, including, without limitation, the rendering of professional services by or through its members, managers, officers or agents, subject to any licensing or registration requirements applicable in any jurisdiction in which the services are rendered or in which such persons are licensed or registered.

General Powers

13. Subject to any limitations provided in this Ordinance or any other law of Nevis or its articles of organization or operating agreement, every limited liability company shall have the same powers as an individual to do all things necessary or convenient in furtherance of its purposes irrespective of company benefit and whether or not enumerated in its articles.

Part III - Registered Agent; Service Of Process

Registered agent for service of process

14.(1) A limited liability company subject to this Ordinance shall at all times have a registered agent in St. Christopher and Nevis. A limited liability company which fails to maintain a registered agent in St. Christopher and Nevis shall be in contravention of this Ordinance.

(2) Service of process on a registered agent may be made by registered mail addressed to the registered agent or any other manner provided by law for the service of summons as if the registered agent were a defendant.

(3) Any registered agent of a limited liability company may resign as such agent upon filing a written notice thereof, executed in duplicate, with the Registrar of Companies, who shall cause a copy thereof to be sent by registered mail to the limited liability company at the address of the office of the company or, if none, at the last known address of a person at whose request the limited liability company was formed. No designation of a new registered agent shall be accepted for filing unless all charges owing to the former agent shall have been paid.

(4) A designation of a registered agent under this section may be made, revoked, or changed by the limited liability company by filing an appropriate notification with the Registrar of Companies.

(5) The designation of a registered agent shall terminate upon the expiration of thirty days written notice of resignation directed to the limited liability company and the filing of a copy of said notice of resignation with the Registrar of Companies; or sooner if a successor agent is designated.

(6) A registered agent, when served process, notice or demand for the limited liability company which he represents, shall transmit the same to the limited liability company by personal notification or in the following manner: Upon receipt of the process, notice or demand, the registered agent shall cause a copy of such paper to be mailed to the limited liability company named therein at its last known address. Such mailing shall be by registered mail. As soon thereafter as possible if process was issued in Nevis, the registered agent may file with the clerk of the court issuing the process either the receipt of such registered mailing or an affidavit stating that such mailing has been made, signed by the registered agent, or if the agent is a corporation, by a properly designated member or manager of the same, properly notarized. Compliance with the provisions of this section shall relieve the registered agent from any further obligation to the limited liability company for service of the process, notice or demand, but the agent's failure to comply with the provisions of this section shall in no way affect the validity of the process, notice or demand.

(7) Only a barrister or solicitor admitted to practice in St. Christopher and Nevis or a corporation having a paid-in capital of at least $500,000.00 may act as registered agent.

(8) No barrister or solicitor or corporation shall act as registered agent unless first licensed by the Minister. The original application for licensing shall be in the prescribed form and accompanied by the prescribed fee and there shall be an annual fee payable in January of each year.

(9) The Minister shall prescribe fees for the licensing of registered agents under this Ordinance.

Registrar of companies or his appointee as agent for process

15.(1) Whenever a limited liability company subject to this Ordinance fails to maintain a registered agent in Nevis, or whenever said registered agent cannot with reasonable diligence be found at his business address, then the Registrar of Companies or his appointee shall be an agent of such limited liability company upon whom any process or notice or demand required or permitted by law to be served may be served.

(2) Service on the Registrar of Companies or his appointee as agent of a limited liability company shall be made by personally delivering to and leaving with him or his deputy or with any person authorized by the Registrar of Companies to receive such service, at the office of the Registrar of Companies, duplicate copies of such process together with the statutory fee. The Registrar of Companies or his appointee shall promptly send one of such copies by registered mail, return receipt requested, to such limited liability company at the business address of its registered agent, or if there is no such office, then the Registrar of Companies or his appointee shall mail such copy in care of any member or manager named in the articles of organization at his address stated therein or at the address of the limited liability company without Nevis, or if none, at the last known address of a person at whose request the limited liability company was formed or in any other manner permitted by law.

Records and certificates of Registrar of Companies

16. The Registrar of Companies shall keep a record of each process served upon the Registrar of Companies or his appointee under this part, including the date of service. It shall, upon request made within five years of such service, issue a certificate under its seal certifying as to the receipt of the process by an authorized person, the date and place of such service, and the receipt of the statutory fee.

Validity of other service

17. Nothing contained in this Part shall affect the validity of service of process on a limited liability company effected in any other manner permitted by law.

PART IV - Relationship Of The Limited Liability Company And Its Members To Third Parties

Effect of organization

18. A limited liability company shall be a legal entity with separate rights and liabilities, distinct from its members or managers. Any estate or interest in property may be acquired, held and conveyed in the name of the limited liability company and title to any estate or interest so acquired vests in the limited liability company.

Liability to third parties

19.(1) The limited liability company shall be solely liable for its own debts, obligations and liabilities.

(2) Notwithstanding any other law, unless liability for limited liability company debts, obligations or liabilities has been assumed by the person against whom liability is asserted pursuant to subsection(3) by such person, no manager, officer, member, employee or agent of a limited liability company, or other person, shall be liable for

(i) limited liability company debts, obligations or liabilities, whether arising in contract, tort or otherwise, solely by reason of being a manager, officer, member, employee or agent of the limited liability company or

(ii) the acts or omissions of any other manager, officer, member, employee or agent of the limited liability company. The failure of a limited liability company to observe the usual company formalities or requirements relating to the exercise of its powers or management of its business is not a ground

for imposing personal liability on the members or managers for liabilities of the company.

(3) Any or all members may assume liability for any or all debts and obligations of the limited liability company.

(4) Nothing in this section shall be interpreted as limiting the criminal liability of any person under any criminal statute.

Limited liability company as proper party to action

20. The limited liability company shall be a proper plaintiff in a suit to assert a legal right of the limited liability company and a proper defendant in a suit to assert a legal right against the limited liability company; and the naming of a member, manager or employee of the limited liability company as a party to a suit in Nevis or elsewhere to represent the limited liability company is subject to a motion to dismiss if such party is the sole party to sue or defend, or subject to a motion for misjoinder if such party is joined with another party who is a proper party and has been joined only to represent the limited liability company.

Part V - Formation Of Limited Liability Companies; Names; Amendment Of Articles Of Organization

Formation

21. One or more persons, without regard to his, their or its residence, domicile, or jurisdiction of organization, may form a limited liability company under this Ordinance by signing and filing articles of organization with the Registrar of Companies in the manner provided in section 4. Such person or persons need not be a member or members of the limited liability company at the time of formation or after formation.

Duration

22. A limited liability company formed under this Ordinance shall have such duration, if any, as shall be stated.

Company Name

23.(1) Except as otherwise provided in subsection (2) of this section, the name of a limited liability company;

>*(a)* Shall contain the words "limited liability company" or the abbreviation "LLC", "L.L.C.", "LC" or "L.C.", and

>*(b)* Shall not be the same as the name of a limited liability company or of any other company of any type or kind, as such name appears on the index of names of existing limited liability companies or companies or on the reserved name list maintained by the Registrar of Companies or a name so similar to any such name as to tend to confuse or deceive.

(2) The provisions of subsection (1) of this section shall not prevent a limited liability company *(a)* with which another limited liability company, domestic or foreign, is merged, or

(b) which is formed by the reorganization or consolidation of one or more domestic or foreign limited liability companies, or

(c) upon a sale, lease or other disposition to or exchange with, a domestic limited liability company of all or substantially all the assets of another domestic limited liability company, including its name, from having the same name as any of such limited liability companies if at the time such other limited liability company was existing under the laws of Nevis.

Register of names

24. The Registrar of Companies shall keep an alphabetical index of all reserved names and those of all limited liability companies subject to this Ordinance together with those other names required to be kept by the Registrar of Companies by law.

Reservation of name

25.(1) Any person or any agent thereof may reserve a name with the Registrar of Companies provided said reservation is made in accordance with this Part and is made in good faith for subsequent use in formation of a limited liability company under this Ordinance or for use in changing the name of a limited liability company already subject to this Ordinance. A name may be reserved under Parts XIII or XIV by a foreign limited liability company which has filed for a transfer of domicile thereunder. Such name reservation shall not be subject to the time limitation and fee requirements of section 25 subsection (4).

(2) An application to reserve a name shall be delivered to the Registrar of Companies together with the required fee. Said application shall set forth:

(a) the name to be reserved;

(b) the name and address of the applicant;

(c) a statement of the reasons for the application in accordance with subsection (1) above; and

(d) the name in which the Certificate of Name Reservation is to be issued.

(3) Provided the name to be reserved is available for use, the Registrar of Companies shall enter the name upon the reserved name list and issue a Certificate of Name Reservation in the name of the applicant or in the name designated by the applicant. The Certificate of Name Reservation shall set forth:

(a) the information contained in the application therefor; and

(b) the date the name was entered upon the reserved name list, which date shall be the date of reservation.

(4) Beginning upon the date of reservation, the name reserved will be maintained upon the reserved name list by the Registrar of Companies and shall not be used except by the person, in whose name the Certificate of Name Reservation has been issued. Said reservation shall terminate upon the expiration of one hundred twenty days next following the date of reservation unless sooner renewed. Upon payment of the required fees, the reservation shall be renewed with the Registrar of Companies for no more than two like periods. An appropriate receipt for the required fees shall be taken along with the Certificate of Name Reservation to be proof of the extension of the reservation.

(5) The Certificate of Name Reservation and any renewals thereof shall be evidenced to the Registrar of Companies at the time the name reserved is utilized by the person, natural or corporate, in whose name said Certificate of Name Reservation has been issued.

Contents of articles of organization.

26. The articles of organization shall set forth:

(a) The name of the limited liability company;

(b) A statement that the limited liability company is formed under this Ordinance;

(c) The latest date on which the limited liability company is to dissolve, if any;

(d) The name and address of the registered agent in Nevis;

(e) Whether the limited liability company is managed by managers exclusive of the members or by all of the members in their capacity as members;

(f) Any provision, not inconsistent with law, which the organizers elect to set forth in the articles of organization for the regulation of the affairs of the limited liability company, and any provision which under this Ordinance is required or permitted to be set forth in the operating agreement.

Execution and filing of articles of organization

27. Articles of organization shall be executed by each person authorized to do so by the persons forming the limited liability company and filed with the Registrar of Companies in conformity with the provisions of Part I of this Ordinance.

Effect of filing articles of organization

28. The limited liability company's existence shall, upon filing the articles of organization, be effective as of the filing date stated thereon. The endorsement by the Registrar of Companies, as required by section 4, shall be conclusive evidence that all conditions precedent required to be performed by the organizers have been complied with and that the limited liability company has been organized under this Ordinance.

Amendment of articles of organization

29.(1) A limited liability company may amend its articles of organization at any time to add or change a provision that is required or permitted in the articles or to delete a provision not required in the articles.

(2) Except as set forth in subsection (3), amendment of the articles of organization shall be subject to the consent of the members entitled to vote thereon.

(3) Any one or more of the following amendments may be approved by the managers without the consent of the members:

(a) To specify or change the location of the office or registered address of the limited liability company; and

(b) To make, revoke or change the designation of a registered agent, or to specify or change the address of its registered agent.

(4) The articles of amendment shall be executed for the limited liability company, acknowledged and filed with the Registrar of

Companies in accordance with the provisions of section 4, and shall set forth:

(a) The name of the limited liability company, and if it has been changed, the name under which it was formed;

(b) The date its articles of organization were filed with the Registrar of Companies;

(c) Each section affected by the amendment.

(5) No amendment shall affect any existing cause of action in favour of or against the limited liability company, or any pending suit to which it shall be a party, or the existing rights of persons other than members; and in the event the limited liability company name shall be changed, no suit brought by or against the limited liability company under its former name shall abate for that reason.

Restated articles of organization

30.(1) At any time after its articles of organization have been amended, a limited liability company may by action of its managers, without necessity of vote of the members, cause to be prepared a document entitled "Restated Articles of Organization", which will integrate into one document its original articles of organization (or articles of consolidation) and all amendments thereto, including those effected by articles of merger.

(2) The restated articles shall also set forth that this document purports merely to restate but not to change the provisions of the original articles of organization as amended and that there is no discrepancy between the said provisions and the provisions of the restated articles.

(3) A copy of the restated articles filed with the Registrar of Companies in the manner provided in section 4 shall be presumed, until otherwise shown, to be the full and true articles of organization as in effect on the date filed.

Operating Agreement

31.(1) The members of a limited liability company may enter into an operating agreement which may contain any provision relating to the business of the limited liability company, the conduct of its affairs, its rights or powers, and the rights of, and its relationship to and among, its members and managers not inconsistent with this Ordinance or any other Law of Nevis or the articles of organization.

(2) An operating agreement shall be agreed to by all members before it becomes effective. The operating agreement shall not require the consent of any future member to remain effective. Unless the articles of organization requires otherwise, an operating agreement need not be in writing.

(3) If the operating agreement does not provide for the method by which it may be amended, then all of the members must agree to any amendment.

(4) A court may enforce an operating agreement by injunction or by granting such other relief that the court in its discretion determines to be fair and appropriate in the circumstances.

(5) The operating agreement may be filed as an exhibit to the articles of organization.

Part VI - Finance

Capital contributions

32. The capital contribution of a member to a limited liability company may be in cash, property, services rendered, or a promissory note or other binding obligation to contribute cash or property or to perform services.

Liability for capital contributors

33.(1) A promise by a member to contribute to the limited liability company is not enforceable unless set forth in a writing signed by the member.

(2) Unless otherwise provided in the operating agreement, a member is obligated to the limited liability company to perform any enforceable promise to contribute cash or property or to perform services.

(3) Except as set forth in subsection(4), if a member for any reason fails to perform any enforceable promise to make the required contribution of property or services, the member is obligated, at the option of the limited liability company, to contribute cash equal to that portion of the value of the stated contribution that has not been made.

(4) If the member is unable to perform an enforceable promise to perform services because of death or disability, the member's estate or other successor is obligated to contribute cash equal to that portion of the value of the stated contribution that has not been made.

(5) An operating agreement may provide that the interest of a member who fails to make a contribution or other payment that the member is required to make shall be subject to specified remedies for, or specified consequences of, the failure in addition to, and not in lieu of, any other rights that the limited liability company may have against such member. The remedy or consequence may take the form of reducing the defaulting member's interest in the limited liability company, subordinating the defaulting member's interest in the limited liability company to that nondefaulting members, a forced sale of the interest in the limited liability company, forfeiture of the interest in the limited liability company, the lending by the nondefaulting members of the amount necessary to meet the commitment, a fixing of the value of the member's interest in the limited liability company by appraisal or by formula and redemption and sale of the member's interest in the limited liability company at that value, or other remedy or consequence.

(6) Unless otherwise provided in the operating agreement, the obligation of a member to make a contribution may be compromised only with the unanimous consent of the members.

Interim Distributions

34. Except as otherwise provided in sections 41 and 57, distributions of cash or other assets of a limited liability company shall be shared among the members, and among classes or groups of members, in the manner and at the times or upon the occurrence of events provided in the operating agreement. If the operating agreement does not so provide, distributions shall be made on the basis of the value of the contributions made by each member to the extent they have been received by the limited liability company and have not been returned.

Distributions in kind prohibited

35. Unless otherwise provided in the operating agreement a member, regardless of the nature of the member's contribution, has no right to demand and receive any distribution from the limited liability company in any form other than cash.

Right to distribution

36. At the time a member becomes entitled to receive a distribution, the member has the status of a creditor of the limited liability company with respect to the distribution.

Part VII - Members And Members' Interests

Admission of members

37.(1) Subject to subsection (2), a person may become a member in a limited liability company:

> *(a)* in the case of a person acquiring an interest in the limited liability company directly from the limited liability company, upon compliance with the operating agreement or, if the operating agreement does not so provide, upon the written consent of all members; and

> *(b)* in the case of an assignee of an interest in the limited liability company, as provided in section 42.

(2) The effective time of admission of a member to a limited liability company shall be the later of:

> *(a)* the date the limited liability company is formed; or

> *(b)* the time provided in the operating agreement or, if no such time is reflected therein, then when the person's admission is reflected in the records of the limited liability company.

(3) A person may be admitted to a limited liability company as a member of a limited liability company and may receive an interest in the limited liability company without making a contribution or being obligated to make a contribution to the limited liability company.

Nature of members' interests

38. A member's interest in the limited liability company is personal property. A member has no interest in specific limited liability company property.

Classes and series of members' interests

39.(1) Members' interests in a limited liability company may be:

(a) of one or more classes or one or more series within any class thereof;

(b) with voting powers, full or limited, or without voting powers;

(c) and with such designations, preferences, rights, qualifications, limitations or restrictions thereon as shall be stated in the operating agreement.

(2) A limited liability company may provide in its operating agreement for one or more classes or series of members' interests which are redeemable, in whole or in part, at the option of the limited liability company at such price or prices, within such period and under such conditions as are stated in the operating agreement.

Termination of a member's interest

40.(1) As used in this section

"Bankruptcy" includes, unless otherwise provided in the operating agreement, a member or manager:

(a) assigning any interest for the benefit of creditors;

(b) filing a voluntary petition in bankruptcy, or its equivalent;

(c) being adjudicated as a bankrupt or as insolvent;

(d) filing a petition or answer seeking any reorganization, arrangement, composition, readjustment, liquidation, dissolution, or similar relief under any statute, law or regulation;

(e) filing an answer or other pleading admitting or failing to contest the material allegations of a petition filed in any proceeding of this nature;

(f) seeking, consenting to, or acquiescing in the appointment of a trustee, receiver, or liquidator of all or any substantial part of his properties;

(g) failing to obtain dismissal within 120 days of any proceeding filed against him seeking any reorganization, arrangement, composition, readjustment, liquidation, dissolution, or similar relief under any statute, law or regulation; or

(h) failing to obtain within 120 days *vacatur* or a stay of the appointment of, or the failure to obtain within 120 days of the date on which the stay was obtained *vacatur* of the appointment of, a trustee, receiver or liquidator of all or any substantial part of his properties.

(2) Unless otherwise provided in the operating agreement, a person ceases to be a member of a limited liability company upon the happening of one of the following termination events:

(a) the member's resignation, expulsion, death, bankruptcy or dissolution, or such other event specified in the operating agreement; or

(b) the member's assignment of his entire interest pursuant to section 42.

(3) Upon the happening of a termination event specified in paragraph (a) of subsection (2), a member shall be treated as having relinquished his member's interest in the limited liability company and shall become an assignee pursuant to subsection (2) of section 42.

(4) Unless provided otherwise in the operating agreement, notwithstanding the termination of a member's interest, no member, assignee or successor to a terminated member may withdraw such member's share of limited liability company capital or other property from the limited liability company nor may he require the limited liability company to acquire his interest prior to dissolution of the limited liability company or the happening of events specified in the operating agreement.

(a) If the member, pursuant to the operating agreement, has the power to withdraw his share of limited liability company capital or other property at specified times or upon the occurrence of specified events, such a withdrawal by a member before the specified time or event is a breach of the operating agreement unless otherwise provided in the operating agreement.

(b) If the member, breaches the operating agreement, or the withdrawal occurs as a result of otherwise wrongful conduct of the member, or the member is expelled for cause, the limited liability company may recover the withdrawing member damages for breach of the operating agreement or as a result of the wrongful conduct or expulsion, including the reasonable costs of obtaining replacement of the services the withdrawn or expelled member was obligated to perform and may offset the damages against the amount otherwise distributable to him, in addition to pursuing any remedies provided for in the operating agreement or otherwise available under applicable law.

(5) Unless provided otherwise in the operating agreement, the pledge of, or granting of a security interest, lien or other encumbrance in or against any or all of a member's interest is not an assignment and shall not cause the member to cease to be a member.

Distributions upon termination of members interests

41. Upon the happening of a termination event that does not cause a dissolution of the limited liability company pursuant to section 51 (1) (c) if the operating agreement provides for a distribution to a terminating member in liquidation of such member's interest in the limited liability company but does not provide the amount of or a method for determining such liquidating distribution to a terminating member, the member shall receive within a reasonable time after termination of his interest the fair market value of the member's interest in the limited liability company as of the date of termination of his interest based upon the net amount which a willing purchaser would pay for the interest to a willing seller, neither being under any compulsion to buy or to sell and both having reasonable knowledge of the relevant facts, but not based solely upon a proportionate value of the underlying assets of the limited liability company.

Assignment of members' interests; restrictions

42.(1) Unless provided otherwise in the operating agreement and subject to the restrictions in subsection (2) a member's interest in a limited liability company is assignable in whole or in part.

(2)*(a)* Unless provided otherwise in the operating agreement, and except as provided in paragraph (b), an assignment does not entitle the assignee to vote on matters on which members may vote, to participate in the management and affairs of the limited liability company or to become, or to exercise any rights of, a member, nor is an assignee responsible for fulfilling fiduciary obligations for which members are responsible, if any. An assignment entitles the assignee to receive, to the extent assigned, only those distributions to which the assignor would be entitled and such share of profits, losses, income, gain, deductions and credits which were allocable to the assignor pursuant to the operating agreement.

(b) Unless provided otherwise in the operating agreement, an assignee of a member's interest may, to the extent assigned, become a member with the full rights and powers of the assignor, and is subject as a member to the same restrictions and liabilities as the assignor, including any liability of the assignor to make capital contributions, if the members other than the assignor and assignee consent to such assignee becoming a member.

(c) The assignor is not released from his liability to make capital contributions to the limited liability company, until such time as the assignee satisfies such requirement.

(3) Unless provided otherwise in the operating agreement, any person becoming entitled by operation of law or otherwise to a member's interest due to the death or incompetency of any member of a limited liability company organized under this Ordinance shall be considered an assignee under this Ordinance and shall have all the right of an assignee of the member's interest. The operating agreement may provide that such person may become a member without consent of the members upon such evidence being produced as may reasonably be required by the managers.

Rights of judgment creditor

43.(1) On application to a court of competent jurisdiction by any judgment creditor of a member of a limited liability company, the court may charge the member's interest with payment of the unsatisfied amount of the judgment with interest. To the extent so charged, the judgment creditor has only the rights of an assignee of the member's interest.

(2) Unless otherwise provided in the operating agreement, the member's interest charged may, but need not, be redeemed at any time:

> *(a)* with separate property of any member, to any one or more of the members; or

> *(b)* with respect to property of the limited liability company, to any one or more of the members whose interests are not charged, on the consent of the members whose interests are not charged, if all members are responsible for management duties pursuant to section 44 (1), or on the consent of the managers whose interests are not charged, if managers are responsible for management duties pursuant to section 44 (2).

(3) Notwithstanding any other law, the remedies provided by subsection (1) shall be the sole remedies available to any creditor of a member's interest.

(4) This Ordinance does not deprive any member of the benefit of any exemption laws applicable to his interest in the limited liability company.

Part VIII - Management

Management of the business of the limited liability company

44.(1) Unless otherwise provided in the operating agreement and subject to subsection (2), management of the business and affairs of a limited liability company shall be vested in all of its members exclusively in their capacity as members.

(2) The operating agreement may fully or partially vest management duties in one or more managers, who may, but need not, be members.

(3) Managers shall have the power to manage the business and affairs of the limited liability company to the extent so vested, exclusive of the members who are not managers.

(4) To the extent not vested in managers as provided in subsection (2), the members in their capacity as members shall retain the power to manage the business and affairs of the limited liability company as set forth in subsection (1).

Voting

45.(1) Unless otherwise provided in this Ordinance or the operating agreement:

> *(a)* if the management of a limited liability company is vested in the members pursuant to subsection 44(1), or where any affirmative consent of the members is required in this Ordinance or the operating agreement, any action required or permitted to be taken by the members shall be taken upon a vote of more than 50% of the members' interests as measured by the members' capital contributions. The measurement of consent set forth in the operating agreement may vary, both in requisite

percentage and in the manner in which it is measured for different purposes. The manner in which consent is measured may refer to, without limitation, the number of members or the proportion, as set forth in the operating agreement, of members' interests in profits, capital or distribution, or any combination thereof.

(b) If the management of a limited liability company is vested in more than one manager pursuant to subsection 44(2), or where any affirmative consent of the managers is required in this Ordinance or the operating agreement, any action required or permitted to be taken by the managers shall be taken upon a vote of a majority of the managers.

(2) Where this Ordinance or the operating agreement requires the consent of the remaining members or remaining managers, as the case may be,

(i) the members' interests of the remaining members shall constitute all of the members' interests entitled to vote thereon, and

(ii) the remaining managers shall constitute all of the managers entitled to vote thereon.

Agency of managers and members

46.(1) Unless otherwise provided in the operating agreement, if management of the limited liability company is vested in the members pursuant to subsection (1) of section 44, each member is an agent of the limited liability company in matters concerning its business or affairs.

(a) An act of a member, including signing of an instrument in the limited liability company name, for apparently carrying on limited

liability company business binds the limited liability company, unless the member had no authority to act for the company in the particular matter and the person with whom the member has dealt knew or had received notice that the member lacked authority; and

(b) An act of a member which is not apparently for carrying on in the ordinary course the limited liability company business of a kind carried on by the limited liability company binds the limited liability company if the act was authorized by the other members.

(2) Unless otherwise provided in the operating agreement, if management of the limited liability company is vested in managers pursuant to subsection (2) of section 44, each manager is an agent of the limited liability company in matters concerning its business.

(a) An act of a manager, including signing of an instrument in the company name, for apparently carrying on company business binds the company, unless the manager had no authority to act for the company in the particular matter and the person with whom the manager has dealt knew or had received notice that the manager lacked authority;

(b) An act of a manager which is not apparently for carrying on in the ordinary course the limited liability company business of a kind carried on by the limited liability company binds the limited liability company if the act was authorized by the other managers;

(c) If management of the limited liability company is vested in managers, no member, solely by reason of being a member, is an agent of the limited liability company.

(3) The operating agreement may provide that acts of members may bind the limited liability company if the managers of the limited liability company are not members but are vested with responsibility for management of the limited liability company solely by contract.

Qualification of managers

47. Unless otherwise provided in the operating agreement, managers may be natural persons, corporations, limited liability companies, partnerships, or other entity, of any nationality and need not be residents of Nevis or members of the limited liability company.

Standard of care to be observed by managers

48. Managers shall discharge the duties of their respective positions in good and with that degree of diligence, care and skill which ordinarily prudent men would exercise under similar circumstances in like positions. In discharging their duties, duly authorized members or managers, as the case may be and officers, when acting in good faith, may rely upon financial statements of the limited liability company represented to them to be correct by the manager of the limited liability company having charge of its books or accounts, or stated in a written report by an independent public or certified public accountant or firm of such accountants fairly to reflect the financial condition of such limited liability company.

Part IX - Relations Of Members And Managers To The Limited Liability Company

Conflicts of interests

49. No contract, loan or other transaction between a limited liability company and one or more of its members or managers, or between a limited liability company and any other person in which one or more of its members or managers are members or managers who have a substantial financial interest, shall be either void or voidable for this reason alone if the material facts as to such member's or manager's interest in such contract or transaction and as to any such common membership, officership or financial interest are disclosed in good faith or known to the limited liability company, and the limited liability company approves such contract or transaction by a vote sufficient for such purpose.

Indemnification of members or managers

50.(1) A limited liability company shall have power to indemnify and hold harmless any person who was or is a party or is threatened to be made a party to any threatened, pending or completed action, suit or proceeding whether civil, criminal, administrative or investigative, including an action by or in the right of the limited liability company, by reason of the fact that he is or was a member or manager of the limited liability company, or is or was serving at the request of the limited liability company as a manager, director, or officer of another person, against expenses (including attorneys' fees), judgments, fines and amounts paid in settlement actually and reasonably incurred by him in connection with such action, suit or proceeding.

(2) To the extent that a member or manager of a limited liability company has been successful on the merits or otherwise in defense of any action, suit or proceeding referred to in subsection (1), or in the defense of a claim, issue or matter therein, he shall be indemnified against expenses (including attorneys' fees) actually and reasonably incurred by him in connection therewith.

(3) Expenses incurred in defending a civil or criminal action, suit or proceeding may be paid in advance of the final disposition of such action, suit or proceeding as authorized by the duly authorized members or managers, as the case may be, in the specific case upon receipt of an undertaking by or on behalf of the member or manager to repay such amount unless it shall ultimately be determined that he is entitled to be indemnified by the limited liability company as authorized in this action.

(4) A limited liability company shall have power to purchase and maintain insurance on behalf of any person who is or was a member or manager of the limited liability company or is or was serving at the request of the limited liability company as a manager, director or officer of another person against any liability asserted against him and incurred by him in such capacity whether or not the limited liability company would have the power to indemnify him against such liability under the provisions of this section.

Part X - Dissolution

When dissolved

51.(1) A limited liability company is dissolved and its affairs shall be wound up upon the happening of the first to occur of the following:

(a) at the time or upon the occurrence of an event specified in writing in the operating agreement;

(b) the written consent of all of the members entitled to vote thereon;

*(c)*unless otherwise provided in the operating agreement, the death, bankruptcy or dissolution (or other event specified in the operating agreement) of

(i) any member of the limited liability company if the limited liability company is managed by the members pursuant to section 44(1), or

(ii) any manager that is also a member of the limited liability company if the limited liability company is managed by managers pursuant to section 44(2), unless the business of the limited liability company is continued by the consent of the remaining members, on or before the 180th day following the occurrence of any such event; or

(d) entry of a decree of judicial dissolution under section 52.

(2) Unless provided otherwise in the operating agreement, an assignment of an interest in a limited liability company does not of itself dissolve the limited liability company.

Judicial dissolution

52. On application by or for a member, the High Court may decree dissolution of a limited liability company whenever it is not reasonably practicable to carry on the business of the limited liability company in conformity with the operating agreement.

Dissolution on failure to pay annual registration fee or appoint registered agent

53.(1) On the failure of a limited liability company to pay the annual registration fee or maintain a registered agent for a period of one year the Registrar shall remove the limited liability company from the register.

(2) A limited liability company is removed from the register pursuant to subsection (1) may be restored to the register within three years of the date of removal upon payment to the Registrar of Companies of the prescribed fee.

(3) A limited liability company shall be restored to the register retroactive to the date of its removal.

(4) Every limited liability company shall pay a fee for restoration to the register.

(5) A limited liability company which is not restored to the register within three years of the date of removal shall be deemed to have commenced to wind up and dissolve in accordance with this part.

Winding up affairs of limited liability company after dissolution

54.(1) All limited liability companies whether they expire by their own limitations or are otherwise dissolved, shall nevertheless be continued for the term of three years from such expiration or dissolution for the purpose of prosecuting and defending suits by or against them, and of enabling them gradually to settle and close their business, to dispose of and convey their property, to discharge their liabilities, and to distribute to the members any remaining assets, but not for the purpose of continuing the business for which the limited liability company was organized. With respect to any action, suit, or proceeding begun by or against the limited liability company either prior to or within three years after the date of its expiration or dissolution, and not concluded within such period, the limited liability company shall be continued beyond that period for the purpose of concluding such action, suit or proceeding and until any judgment, order, or decree therein shall be fully executed.

(2) Upon the dissolution of any limited liability company, the managers shall be trustees thereof, with full power to settle the affairs, collect the outstanding debts, sell and convey the property, real and personal, as may be required by the laws of the jurisdiction where situated, prosecute and defend all such suits as may be necessary or proper for the purposes aforesaid, distribute the money and other property among the members after paying or adequately providing for payment of its liabilities and obligations, and do all other acts which might be done by the limited liability company, before dissolution, that may be necessary for the final settlement of the unfinished business of the limited liability company.

(3) At any time within three years after the filing of the articles of dissolution, the High Court, in a special proceeding instituted under this section, upon the petition of the limited liability company, or of a creditor, claimant, manager, member, or organizer or any other person in interest, may continue the liquidation of the limited liability company under the supervision of the court in Nevis and may make all such orders as it may deem proper in all matters in connection with the dissolution or in winding up the affairs of the limited liability

company, including the appointment or removal of a receiver, who may be a manager or member of the limited liability company.

Agency power of managers after dissolution

55.(1) Except as provided in subsections (3) and (4), after dissolution of the limited liability company, each of the managers having authority to wind up the limited liability company's business and affairs can bind the limited liability company:

> *(a)* by any act appropriate for winding up the limited liability company's affairs or completing transactions unfinished at dissolution; and

> *(b)* by any transaction that would have bound the limited liability company if it had not been dissolved, if the other party to the transaction does not have notice of the dissolution.

(2) The filing of the articles of dissolution shall be presumed to constitute notice of dissolution for purposes of subsection (1)(b).

(3) An act of a manager which is not binding on the limited liability company pursuant to subsection (1) is binding if it is otherwise authorized by the limited liability company.

(4) An act which would be binding under subsection (1) or would be otherwise authorized but which is in contravention of a restriction on authority shall not bind the limited liability company to persons having a knowledge of the restriction.

Settlement of claims against limited company

56.(1) Any time within one year after dissolution, a limited liability company may give notice requiring all creditors and claimants, including any with unliquidated or contingent claims and any with whom the limited liability company has unfulfilled contracts, to present their claims in writing and in detail at a specified place and by a specified day, which shall not be less than 120 days after the first publication of such notice.

> *(a)* Notice shall be published at least once a week for four successive weeks in a newspaper of general circulation in Nevis.

> *(b)* On or before the date of the first publication of notice, the limited liability company shall mail a copy thereof, postage prepaid and addressed to his last known address, to each person known to be a creditor of or claimant against the limited liability company whose name and address are known to the limited liability company.

(2) The giving of notice shall not constitute a recognition that any person is a proper creditor or claimant, and shall not revive or make valid or operate as a recognition of the validity of, or a waiver of any defense or counter claim in respect of any claim against the limited liability company, its assets, managers or members, which has been barred by any statute of limitation or which has become invalid by any cause, or in respect of which the limited liability company, its members or managers have any defense or counterclaim.

(3) Any claims which shall have been filed as provided in such notice and which shall be disputed by the limited liability company may be submitted for determination to the High Court.

(4) Any person whose claim is, at the date of the first publication of the notice, barred by any statute of limitations is not a creditor or claimant entitled to any notice under this section. The claim of any such person and all other claims which are not timely filed as provided in the notice except claims which are the subject of litigation on the date of the first publication of such notice, and all claims which are so filed but are disallowed by the High Court, shall be forever barred as against the limited liability company, its assets, members or managers except to such extent, if any, as the High Court may allow them against any remaining assets of the limited liability company in the case of the creditor who shows satisfactory reason for his failure to file his claim as so provided.

(5) Notwithstanding anything in this section, tax claims and other claims by the Nevis Island Government shall not be required to be filed under this Ordinance, and such claims shall not be barred because not so filed, and distribution of the assets of the limited liability company, or any part thereof, may be deferred until determination of any such claims.

Distribution of assets upon winding up

57. Upon the winding up of a limited liability company, the assets shall be distributed as follows:

> *(a)* payment, or adequate provision for payment, shall be made to creditors, including, to the extent permitted by law, members who are creditors in satisfaction of liabilities of the limited liability company;

> *(b)* unless otherwise provided in the operating agreement, to members or former members in satisfaction of liabilities for distributions; and

> *(c)* unless otherwise provided in the operating agreement, to members and former members first for the return of their contributions and second in proportion to the members' shares of distributions from the limited liability company prior to dissolution.

Articles of dissolution

58.(1) After dissolution of the limited liability company pursuant to section 52, the limited liability company may file articles of dissolution with the Registrar of Companies in accordance with the provisions of section 4.

(2) The articles of dissolution shall set forth:

(a) the name of the limited liability company;

(b) the date its articles of organization, and all amendments thereto, were filed with the Registrar of Companies;

(c) the name and address of each of its managers having authority to wind up the limited liability company's business and affairs; and

(d) the reason for the dissolution.

Part XI - Conversion; Merger And Consolidation

Conversion of a corporation to a limited liability company

59.(1) Whenever used in this section and in section 60, "corporation" means a corporation formed under the Nevis Business Corporation Ordinance or redomiciled in Nevis.

(2) A plan of conversion must set forth the terms and conditions of the conversion of the interests of the shareholders of the corporation into interests in the limited liability company or the cash or other consideration to be paid or delivered as a result of the conversion.

(3) The terms and conditions of a conversion of a corporation to a limited liability company must be approved by the corporation in the manner required by the Nevis Business Corporation Ordinance, its articles of incorporation or bylaws.

(4) After the plan is approved in accordance with subsection 3 the corporation shall file articles of organization with the Registrar of Companies in the manner set forth in Part V. In addition to the requirements of Part V, the articles of organization shall include:

(a) the name of the corporation from which the limited liability company was converted;

(b) a statement that all requirements of the Nevis Business Corporation Ordinance have been satisfied;

(5) The filing of the articles of organization cancels the certificate of incorporation as of the effective date of the articles of organization.

(6) A person who has personal liability for debts and obligations of the corporation which was converted to the limited liability company, remains liable for debts and obligations incurred by the corporation before the effective date of the formation of the converted limited liability company to the same extent as he would be liable had there not been a conversion.

(7) A person's liability for debts and obligations of the limited liability company incurred on or after the effective date of the formation of the converted limited liability company is that of a member of a limited liability company as provided in this Ordinance.

Effect of conversion

60.(1) A corporation that has been converted pursuant to this Part is for purposes the same entity that existed before the conversion.

(2) When a conversion takes effect:

(a) all property owned by the converting corporation is vested in the limited liability company without further act or deed. If deeds or other documents evidencing ownership or title must be filed in any jurisdiction, such documents shall be filed only to give notice that the name and form of owner of such property has been changed, and not to evidence or record a change of owner or title holder;

(b) all debts, liabilities and other obligations of the converting corporation continue as obligations of the limited liability company;

(c) an action or proceeding pending by or against the converting corporation may be continued as if the conversion had not occurred, except that, if appropriate in the jurisdiction in which the proceeding is pending, the caption of the action may be changed to reflect the conversion;

(d) notwithstanding an other law, all the rights, privileges, immunities, powers and purposes of the converting corporation are vested in the limited liability company; and

(e) except as otherwise provided in the plan of conversion, all of the shareholders of the converting corporation continue as members of the limited liability company.

Merger or Consolidation

61.(1) Whenever used in this part:

"**consolidation**" means a procedure whereby any one or more limited liability companies consolidate with other limited liability companies or with other business entities into a new domestic limited liability company or other business entity formed by the consolidation

"**merger**" means a procedure whereby any one or more limited liability companies merge with or into other limited liability companies or other business entities to form a single limited liability company, which is any one of the parties to the merger

"**other business entity**" means a corporation, association, a real estate investment trust, or any other unincorporated business, including a partnership, a limited partnership, and a limited life company, whether foreign or domestic, and a foreign limited liability company, but excluding a domestic limited liability company.

(2) Pursuant to a plan of merger, a domestic limited liability company may be merged or consolidated with or into one or more domestic limited liability companies or other business entities, with one domestic limited liability company or other business entity as the plan shall provide being the surviving or consolidated limited liability company or other business entity.

(3) In the case where one or more parties to the merger or consolidation are other business entities formed in a foreign jurisdiction such entities may be merged or consolidated with one or more domestic limited liability companies if such merger or consolidation is permitted by the laws of the jurisdiction under which each such other business entity is established.

(4) The plan of merger or consolidation must set forth:

(a) the name and jurisdiction of formation of each entity that is a party to the merger;

(b) the name and address of the surviving or consolidated limited liability company or other business entity;

(c) the type of organization of the surviving or consolidated entity;

(d) the terms and conditions of the proposed merger or consolidation, including the manner and basis of converting the interests of each party to the merger or consolidation into interests, bonds or other securities of the surviving or consolidated entity, or the cash or other consideration to be paid or delivered in exchange for such interests, or a combination thereof.

(5) In the case of a domestic limited liability company that is a party to the merger or consolidation, unless a greater quantity is otherwise required in the operating agreement, the plan of merger or consolidation shall be consented to by the members of such domestic limited liability company who are entitled to vote thereon.

All other parties must authorize the merger or consolidation pursuant to the laws applicable thereto.

(6) After approval of the plan of merger or consolidation, but before it takes effect, the plan may be terminated or amended pursuant to a provision for such termination or amendment within the plan.

(7) After approval of the plan of merger or consolidation, articles of merger or consolidation shall be executed in duplicate on behalf of each limited liability company and other business entity that is party to the merger or consolidation and shall set forth:

(a) the plan of merger or consolidation that had been duly approved as set forth herein, and, in case a domestic limited liability company is the surviving or consolidated entity, any statement required to be included in articles of organization for a limited liability company formed under this Ordinance;

(b) for each domestic limited liability company party to the merger or consolidation, the date the articles of organization of each such domestic limited liability company were filed with the Registrar of Companies;

(c) the effective date of the merger or consolidation, subject to subsection (1) of section 62, if not effective upon filing; and

(d) the manner in which the merger or consolidation was authorized with respect to each party to the merger or consolidation.

(8) The articles of merger or articles of consolidation shall be filed with the Registrar of Companies in accordance with the provisions of section 4.

(9) If the surviving or consolidated limited liability company is to be governed by the laws of any jurisdiction other than Nevis:

(a) it shall file with the Registrar of Companies a certificate of merger or consolidation issued by the appropriate official of the foreign jurisdiction;

(b) the effect of such merger or consolidation shall be the same as in the case of the merger or consolidation of domestic limited liability companies except in so far as the laws of such other jurisdiction provide otherwise;

(c) the effective date of a merger or consolidation shall be determined by the filing requirements and laws of such other jurisdiction.

Effect of merger or consolidation

62.(1) The merger or consolidation shall be effective upon the filing of the articles of merger or consolidation with the Registrar of Companies or on such date subsequent thereto, not to exceed thirty days, as shall be set forth in such articles.

(2) When a merger or consolidation has been effected and the surviving or consolidated entity is a domestic limited liability company:

(a) such surviving or consolidated domestic limited liability company shall thereafter consistent with its articles of organization as altered or established by the merger or consolidation, possess all the rights, privileges, immunities, powers and purposes of each of the parties to the merger or consolidation;

(b) all the property, real and personal, including causes of action and every other asset of each of the parties to the merger or consolidation shall vest in such surviving or consolidated domestic limited liability company without further act or deed;

(c) the surviving or consolidated domestic limited liability company shall assume and be liable for all the liabilities, obligations and penalties of each of the parties to the merger or consolidation. No liability or obligation due or to become due, claim or demand for any cause existing against any such party shall be released or impaired by such merger or consolidation. No action or proceeding, whether civil or criminal, then pending by or against any such party to the merger or consolidation shall abate or be discontinued by such merger or consolidation, but may be enforced, prosecuted, settled or compromised as if such merger or consolidation had not occurred, or such surviving or consolidated limited liability company may be substituted in such action or special proceeding in place of any party to the merger or consolidation;

(d) in the case of a merger, the articles of organization of the surviving limited liability company shall be automatically amended to the extent, if any, that changes in its articles of organization are set forth in the plan of merger; and, in the case of consolidation, the statements set forth in the articles of consolidation and which are required or permitted to be set forth in the articles of organization of a limited liability company formed under this Ordinance, shall be its articles of organization; and

(e) unless otherwise provided in the articles of merger or consolidation, all parties to the merger or consolidation which is not the surviving domestic limited liability company or the consolidated domestic limited liability company, ceases to exist and is dissolved.

Sale, lease exchange or other disposition of assets

63. Unless otherwise specified in the operating agreement, the manager of a limited liability company may sell, lease, exchange or dispose of all or substantially all the assets of a limited liability company, whether or not made in the usual or regular course of the business actually conducted by such limited liability company.

Part XII - Transfer Of Domicile To Nevis

Definitions

64. As used in this Part and Part XIV, unless the context otherwise requires, the term:

"**Foreign Domicile**" means a jurisdiction other than Nevis in which a limited liability company has been formed.

"**Articles of Organization**" means such document filed in the Foreign Domicile that serves the same purposes as does articles of organization in Nevis

When transfer of domicile is permitted

65.(1) Any Foreign Limited Liability Company may, subject to and upon compliance with the further provisions of this Part, transfer its domicile into Nevis, and may perform the acts described in the provisions of this Part, transfer its domicile into Nevis, and may perform the acts described in the provisions of this Part, so long as the law of the Foreign Domicile do not expressly prohibit such transfer.

(2) Nothing in this Ordinance shall be regarded as permitting a Foreign Limited Liability Company which transfers its domicile to Nevis to transfer business operations to Nevis.

Application to transfer Domicile

66. Any Foreign Limited Liability Company may apply for permission to transfer its domicile to Nevis by filing with the Registrar of Companies an Application to Transfer Domicile which shall be executed in accordance with section 68 and filed and recorded in accordance with section 4, together with:

(a) a certificate evidencing its existence issued by an authorized officer of the Foreign Domicile; and

(b) a certified copy of the Articles of Organization, with amendments, if any, and if said documents are not in English, translation thereof under oath of the translator.

Contents of Application to Transfer Domicile

67. An application to transfer Domicile must contain:

(a) the date on which, and the jurisdiction where, the Foreign Limited Liability Company was formed, organized, created or otherwise came into existence; and

(b) the name of the Foreign Limited Liability Company;

(c) the name the Foreign Limited Liability Company will be adopting upon re-domiciliation in Nevis;

(d) a declaration that the transfer of domicile has been approved by all necessary action of the managers;

(e) a declaration that the transfer of domicile is made in good faith and will not serve to hinder, delay or defraud existing members, creditors, claimants or other parties in interest;

(f) the name and address of the limited liability company's registered agent in Nevis;

(g) any other pertinent information required to be set forth in articles of organization under section 26; and

(h) the amendments of its Articles of Organization or their equivalent, that are to be effective upon filing the application to transfer domicile.

Execution of the Application to Transfer Domicile

68. The Application to Transfer Domicile shall be in English and notwithstanding the requirements of section 4(3) of this Ordinance, shall be signed by a manager of the limited liability company or any other person performing functions equivalent to those of a manager, however named or described and who is authorized to sign such Application to Transfer Domicile on behalf of the limited liability company.

Transfer of domicile to Nevis; Certificate of Transfer of Domicile

69. Upon the filing of the Application to Transfer Domicile and the documents referred to in sections 66 and 67, together with the fees prescribed in section 6, if the Registrar of Companies shall find that such documents are in proper form and satisfy the requirements of this Part, and if the name of the limited liability company meets the requirements of section 23, then the Registrar of Companies shall deliver to the limited liability company a Certificate of Transfer of Domicile and the limited liability company shall become domiciled and domesticated in Nevis as a limited liability company of Nevis and shall thereafter be subject to all provisions of this Ordinance, and the limited liability company shall be deemed to have commenced its existence on the date the limited liability company was first formed, organized, created or otherwise came into existence and shall be deemed to have continued its existence in Nevis, and thereafter. The limited liability company shall promptly adapt its operating agreement, its registration, management and records to comply with Nevis Law.

Prior obligations and liabilities

70.(1) A Foreign Limited Liability Company that has been re-domiciled pursuant to this Part is for all purposes the same entity that existed before the re-domiciliation.

(2) When a re-domiciliation takes effect:

(a) all property owned by the re-domiciliating Foreign Limited Liability Company is vested in the limited liability company without further act or deed. If deeds or other documents evidencing ownership or title must be filed in any jurisdiction, such document shall be filed only to give notice that the name and form of owner of such property has been changed, and not to evidence or record a change of owner or title holder;

(b) all debts, liabilities and other obligations of the re-domiciliating Foreign Limited Liability Company continue as obligations of the limited liability company;

(c) an action or proceeding pending by or against the re-domiciliating Foreign Limited Liability Company may be continued as if the re-domiciliation had not occurred, except that, if appropriate in the jurisdiction in which the proceeding is pending, the caption of the action may be changed to reflect the re-domiciliation;

(d) except as prohibited by other law, all the rights, privileges, immunities, powers and purposes of the re-domiciliating Foreign Limited Liability Company are vested in the limited liability company; and

(e) all of the members of the re-domiciliating Foreign Limited Liability Company continue as members of the limited liability company.

(3) The transfer of domicile of any Foreign Limited Liability Company to Nevis shall not be deemed to affect any obligations or liabilities of said Foreign Limited Liability Company incurred prior to such transfer.

Applicable law

71. The filing of an Application to Transfer Domicile shall not affect the choice of law applicable to prior obligations and rights of the limited liability company, except that from the date the Application to Transfer Domicile is filed, the laws of Nevis, including the provisions of this Ordinance, shall apply to the limited liability company to the same extent as if the limited liability company had been originally organized as a limited liability company of Nevis on that date and title to the limited liability company's assets shall also be governed by Nevis law.

Part XIII - Transfer Of Domicile From Nevis

Departure

72. Any limited liability company formed, organized, created, or otherwise existing under or subject to this Ordinance may become domiciled in any foreign jurisdiction upon compliance with this Ordinance and the laws of the jurisdiction into which the limited liability company seeks to become domiciled.

Certificate of departure

73. Any limited liability company described in section 72 shall submit for filing with the Registrar of Companies a Certificate of Departure which shall be executed in the same manner as an Application to Transfer Domicile. The Certificate of Departure shall set forth:

> *(a)* The names and addresses of the limited liability company's creditors and the total amount of its indebtedness to such creditors, and the names and addresses of all persons or entities which have notified the limited liability company in writing of a claim in excess of one thousand dollars and the total amount of such claims;

> *(b)* That the intended departure from Nevis and transfer of domicile to a foreign jurisdiction is unlikely to be detrimental to the rights or property interests of any creditor of or claimant against the limited liability company;

> *(c)* That the limited liability company at the time of application to the foreign jurisdiction is not in breach of any duty or obligation imposed upon it by this Ordinance or any other law of Nevis;

(d) That the transfer of domicile to the foreign jurisdiction is made in good faith and will not serve to hinder, delay or defraud existing members or other parties in interest;

(e) A consent and agreement by the limited liability company that it may be served with process in Nevis in any proceeding arising out of actions or omissions occurring prior to its departure from Nevis, which agreement shall include the appointment of the Registrar of Companies as the agent of the limited liability company to accept such service of process and shall set forth an address to which a copy of such process shall be forwarded by mail.

Effective date of departure

74. Upon payment of all fees outstanding in Nevis and upon proper compliance with this Ordinance and applicable laws for transfer of domicile to the foreign jurisdiction, the departing limited liability company shall notify the Registrar of Companies as to the effective date of the transfer of domicile outside of Nevis. As of the date of such transfer to the foreign jurisdiction, said limited liability company shall be deemed to have ceased to be a limited liability company domiciled in Nevis.

Jurisdiction of courts after departure

75. Nothing in this Part shall obviate, diminish or affect the jurisdiction of any court in Nevis to hear and determine any proceeding commenced therein by or against the limited liability company arising out of actions or omissions which occurred before the limited liability company ceased to be domiciled in Nevis.

Part XIV - Emergency Transfer Of Domicile Into Nevis

Emergency conditions

76. As used in this Part, unless the context requires otherwise, the term:

"**Emergency condition**" shall be deemed to include but not be limited to any of the following: war or other armed conflict; revolution or insurrection; invasion or occupation by foreign military forces; rioting or civil commotion of an extended nature; domination by a foreign power; expropriation, nationalization or confiscation of a material part of the assets or property of the limited liability company; impairment of the institution of private property (including private property held abroad); the taking of any action under the laws of Nevis whereby persons resident in the Foreign Domicile might be treated as "enemies" or otherwise restricted under the law of Nevis relating to trading with enemies of Nevis; or the immediate threat of any of the foregoing; and such other event which, under the laws of the Foreign Domicile permits the limited liability company to transfer its domicile. Terms used in this Part and not defined herein are used as defined in section 64.

When emergency transfer of domicile is permitted

77. During the existence of an Emergency Condition in the jurisdiction of its domicile any Foreign Limited Liability Company may, subject to and upon compliance with the further provisions of this Part, apply for an emergency transfer of its domicile to Nevis.

Application for emergency transfer of domicile

78.(1) Any Foreign Limited Liability Company may apply for emergency transfer of domicile to Nevis by filing with the Registrar of Companies:

(a) documents and certificates similar in respect to those required by sections 66 and 67, except that such documents shall refer to an emergency transfer of domicile pursuant to this Part; and

(b) a certificate of an authorized office, director or agent of the Foreign Limited Liability Company specifying the Emergency Condition which exists in the Foreign Domicile.

(2) The Registrar of Companies, in his discretion, may waive any of the above requirements upon request by such limited liability company supported by facts (including without limitation, the existence of an Emergency Condition) justifying such waiver. In addition, if Emergency Conditions have affected ordinary means of communication, any of the documents or certificates hereby required may be submitted by telegram, telex, telecopy or other form of writing so long as the duly executed original documents and supporting documentation are received by the Registrar of Companies within 30 days thereafter or as soon as the Emergency conditions cease to exist. If the Registrar of Companies finds the required documents and certificates to be in proper form upon payment of the prescribed fee, the Registrar of Companies shall certify that the limited liability company has filed all documents and paid all fees required by this Part, and shall deliver to the Foreign Limited Liability Company a Certificate of Transfer of Domicile, and such certificate of the Registrar of Companies shall be prima facie evidence of the transfer by such limited liability company of its domicile into Nevis.

Governing law after emergency transfer

79. Except to the extent expressly prohibited by the laws of Nevis after a Foreign Limited Liability Company transfers its domicile to Nevis pursuant to this Part, the limited liability company shall have all of the powers which it had immediately prior to such transfer under the laws of the Foreign Domicile and the managers of the limited liability company and their successors may manage the business and affairs of the limited liability company in accordance with the laws of such jurisdiction.

Prior obligations and liabilities

80. The emergency transfer by any limited liability company of its domicile into Nevis pursuant to this Part shall not be deemed to affect any obligations or liabilities of such limited liability company incurred prior to such transfer.

Service of process after emergency transfer of domicile

81. All process issued out of any court of Nevis, all orders made by any court of Nevis, and all rules and notices of any kind required to be served on any limited liability company which has transferred its domicile into Nevis pursuant to this Part may be served on the limited liability company and its managers pursuant to section 15 in the same manner as if such limited liability company were a limited liability company of Nevis.

Return to foreign jurisdiction

82. Any limited liability company which has transferred its domicile into Nevis pursuant to this Part may return to the Foreign Domicile by filing with the Registrar of Companies a Certificate of Departure pursuant to sections 72 and 73. Such application shall be accompanied by a certified resolution of the managers of the limited liability company authorizing such withdrawal.

Part XV - Tax Exemption

Exemption

83.(1) Any limited liability company subject to this Ordinance which does no business in Nevis shall not be subject to any corporate tax, income tax, withholding tax, stamp tax, asset tax, exchange controls, or other fees or taxes based upon or measured by assets or income originating outside of Nevis or in connection with other activities outside of Nevis or in connection with matters of corporate administration which may occur in Nevis, except as provided in sections 6 and 7.

(2) For purposes of this section, no limited liability company shall be considered to be doing business in Nevis solely because it engages in one or more of the following activities:

(a) maintaining bank accounts in Nevis;

(b) holding meetings of managers or members in Nevis;

(c) maintaining company or financial records in Nevis;

(d) maintaining an administrative or managerial office in Nevis with respect to assets or activities outside of Nevis;

(e) maintaining a registered agent in Nevis;

(f) investing in stocks or interests of Nevis corporations or limited liability companies or being a partner in a Nevis partnership or a beneficiary of a Nevis trust or estate.

Licence required for management office

83A.(1) Notwithstanding subsection (2)(d) of section 83, no limited liability company shall maintain an administrative or management office in Nevis unless licensed to do so by the Minister of Finance.

(2) An application for a licence shall be in such form as may be prescribed or, until a form is prescribed, in such form as the Minister of Finance may require and shall be accompanied by such particulars and such evidence, documentary or otherwise, as the Minister of Finance requires.

(3) A licence may be issued subject to such conditions or restrictions as the Minister of Finance thinks fit to impose.

(4) A licence may be revoked by the Minister of Finance on the breach of any condition or restriction to which the licence is subject.

(5) Any limited liability company that maintains an administrative or management office in Nevis without a licence shall be subject to a fine of $50,000 and to be struck off the register.

(6) The provisions of this section shall apply to every limited liability company that -

(a) maintains an administrative or management office in Nevis immediately before the commencement of this Ordinance; or

(b) wishes to maintain an administrative or management office in Nevis on or after the commencement of this Ordinance.

(7) A limited liability company described in subsection (6)(a) may apply for a licence within 30 days after the commencement of this Ordinance and shall not be deemed to be in violation of this Ordinance during such period that the application is being considered by the Minister of Finance.

(8) If an application made by a limited liability company under subsection (7) is rejected the corporation shall close its offices in Nevis within 10 days after receipt of the notice of rejection.

Limitation of section 83A.

83B. The provisions of section 83A shall not apply to any limited liability company that is managed or administered by a company or a person duly licensed by the Minister of Finance in accordance with Section 14 of the principal Ordinance or in accordance with any other law enacted by the Nevis Island Legislature.

Dividends and distributions

84. In addition, any dividend or distribution by limited liability companies, corporations or other entities which do no business in Nevis or to individuals who are not citizens or residents of Nevis, shall be exempt from any tax or withholding provisions of Nevis law which would otherwise be applicable to such limited liability company making the distribution or allocation or the recipient of the distribution or allocation.

Part XVI - Miscellaneous

Savings provisions

85. This Ordinance shall not affect any cause of action, liability, penalty, or action or special proceeding which on the effective date of this Ordinance is accrued, existing, incurred or pending, but the same may be asserted, enforced, prosecuted, or defended as if this Ordinance had not been enacted.

Regulations

86.(1) The Minister may make regulations with respect to the duties to be performed by the Registrar of Companies under this Ordinance.

(2) Without limiting or affecting subsection (1), the Minister may make regulations with respect to the conduct, duties and responsibilities of registered agents.

Endorsement Certificate

87. Upon the filing of any instrument the Registrar of Companies shall issue a certificate of endorsement under his hand and seal certifying that the instrument is filed.

Certificate of Good Standing

88. The Registrar of Companies shall, upon request by any registered agent, issue a certificate of Good Standing under his hand and seal certifying that a limited liability company subject to this Ordinance is of good standing if he is satisfied that -

> *(a)* the name of the limited liability company is on the register; and

(b) the limited liability company has paid all fees required under this Ordinance; and

(c) the limited liability company is not in contravention of any of the provisions of this Ordinance or is in the process of being wound up and dissolved.

Form of certificate

89. Any certificate or other document required to be issued by the Registrar of Companies under this Ordinance shall be in such form as the Minister may approve.

NEVIS OFFSHORE BANKING ORDINANCE 1996

Preliminary

Short title

1. This Ordinance may be cited as the Nevis Offshore Banking Ordinance, 1996.

Interpretation

2. In this Ordinance

"**auditor**" means an auditor described in section 43 and includes a partnership of auditors.

"**business**" in relation to a licensee means offshore banking business of the licensee;

"**director**," means a director within the meaning of section 32;

"**licensee**" means a body corporate that holds a subsisting licence under this Ordinance to carry on an offshore banking business from within Nevis;

"**Minister**" means the Minister responsible for Finance in the Nevis Island Administration;

"**offshore banking**" has the meaning given that expression in section 4;

"**permanent secretary**" means the permanent secretary in the Ministry of Finance in the Nevis Island Administration;

"**prescribed**" means prescribed by regulations;

"**share**" in relation to a company includes stock of the company.

(2) A reference in this Ordinance to a resident of Nevis refers to a person described in section 86, and a reference to a person resident outside Nevis refers to a person described in section 87.

Purposes of Ordinance

3.(1) The purposes of this Ordinance are

(a) to encourage the development of Nevis as a responsible offshore financial centre;

(b) to provide incentives by way of tax reduction, exemptions and benefits for offshore banking carried on from within Nevis; and

(2) This Ordinance shall receive such fair and liberal construction interpretation as will best ensure the attainment of its purposes.

Part I - Offshore Banking

Offshore banking

4.(1) Offshore banking is

(a) receiving foreign funds through

(i) the acceptance of foreign money deposits payable upon receipt demand or after a fixed period or after notice,

(ii) the sale or placement of foreign bonds, certificates, notes or other debt obligations or other securities, or

(iii) any other similar activities involving foreign money or foreign securities, and

(b) either in whole or in part using foreign funds so acquired for loans, advances and investments whether in Nevis or elsewhere.

(2) Offshore banking also includes, for the purpose of this Ordinance, any other activity, which the minister may, by regulations, declare to be an activity related or ancillary to an activity described in subsection (1).

Prohibition without licence

5. No person shall engage in offshore banking in or from within Nevis at any time when he is not a licensee.

Issue of licences.

6. No licence may be issued under this Ordinance to any person other than an eligible company or qualified foreign bank.

Eligible company

7.(1) A body corporate is an eligible company if it is a wholly owned subsidiary of a local bank regulated by the Eastern Caribbean Central Bank that is licensed under the Banking Act to do banking business in Nevis.

(2) For the purposes of subsection (1) a local bank means a bank indigenous to St. Kitts and Nevis.

Qualified foreign bank

8. A qualified foreign bank is

(a) a foreign bank that upon the commencement of this Ordinance is licensed under the Banking Act,

(b) a foreign bank with minimum capitalisation and assets, as prescribed by the Minister, that is not licensed under the Banking Act but is licensed to do domestic banking in its jurisdiction of incorporation,

(c) a financial institution, approved by the Minister, that is directly or indirectly a wholly owned foreign subsidiary within the meaning of section 13(6), of a foreign bank described in paragraph (a) or (b) above.

Part II - Licensing Requirements

Consent of Minister

9.(1) Notwithstanding the Companies Act, no company may be incorporated under that Act for the purpose of doing offshore banking from within Nevis unless its incorporation has or been consented to by the Minister.

(2) Notwithstanding anything in its memorandum or articles of association, no company incorporated under the Companies Act before the commencement of this Ordinance has capacity to do offshore banking from within Nevis unless its memorandum and articles of association are, or are amended, to the satisfaction of the Minister.

Application requirements

10.(1) An eligible company must

(a) be incorporated under the Companies Act as a company limited by shares,

(b) have objects or business activities restricted to off-shore banking from within Nevis,

(c) have at least one director who is a citizen of St. Kitts and Nevis with a residence in Nevis;

(d) have memorandum and articles of association acceptable to the Minister,

(e) have authorised and paid up capital in accordance with the requirements of section 22.

(2) Every applicant for a licence under this Ordinance must *(a)* show that it is an eligible company or a qualified foreign bank,

(b) give the names and address of its directors,

(c) give particulars of the off-shore banking it proposes to do from within Nevis,

(d) give the names of any shareholders who are residents of Nevis and the number of shares held directly or indirectly by residents of Nevis, and

(e) provide such other information of a financial or other nature as the Minister may require in any particular case.

(3) An application for a licence by an eligible company must be accompanied by a certified copy of the memorandum and articles of association of the applicant.

(4) An application for a licence and all documents submitted pursuant to this Ordinance in support of the application must be signed by the directors of the company making the application.

(5) An application for a licence by a qualified foreign bank must be accompanied by such documents as are prescribed by the Minister.

Tentative applicants

11.(1) Any person who intends to apply for a licence under this Ordinance may submit a proposal to the Minister for a licence, and the Minister may indicate whether or not a subsequent application based on the proposal would be favourably received by him.

(2) Nothing done by the Minister under subsection (1) precludes him from later refusing an application for a licence that was based on a proposal considered by him pursuant to that section on grounds that the applicant withheld material information or that the proposed application was made in bad faith.

Director's qualification

12. Where a company has appointed a citizen of St. Kitts and Nevis who is a resident of Nevis to its board of directors under this Ordinance, that director need not subscribe for nor acquire any shares of the company.

Examination of applicants

13.(1) On receipt of an application for a licence under this Ordinance, the Minister may cause such investigation to be made of the applicant, its financial circumstances, and any associates or affiliates of the applicant, as the Minister considers necessary in the public interest.

(2) In particular, the Minister shall require an examination to be made of

(a) the financial status and history of the applicant and any of its directors associates or affiliates,

(b) the character and experience of the directors thereof,

(c) the adequacy of its capital for the purpose of the business it intends to carry on,

(d) the needs of the public or persons it intends to serve, and

(e) its earning prospects and its prospects as an employer.

(3) For the purposes of this section, "associate" means, when used to indicate a relation with any person

(a) a company of which that person beneficially owns or controls, directly or indirectly, shares or securities convertible into shares carrying more than ten per cent of the voting rights under all

circumstances or by reason of occurrence of an event that has occurred and is continuing, or a currently exercisable option or right to purchase those shares or convertible securities;

(b) a partner of that person acting on behalf of the partnership of which they are partners;

(c) a trust or estate in which that person has a substantial beneficial interest or in respect of which he serves as a trustee or in a similar capacity;

(d) a spouse or a child of that person; or

*(e)*a relative of that person or of the spouse of that person if the relative has the same residence as that person.

(4) For the purpose of this section

(a) one company is affiliated with another company if one of them is the subsidiary of the other or both are subsidiaries of the same holding company or each of them is controlled by the same person;

(b) if two companies are affiliated with the same company at the same time, they are affiliated with each other at that time.

(5) A company is the holding company of another if that other company is its subsidiary.

(6) A company is a subsidiary of another company if it is controlled by that other company.

Duty to issue or refuse licence

14.(1) It is the duty of the Minister to issue or refuse a licence under this Ordinance to an applicant.

(a) within three months of the receipt of the application, or

(b) if additional information is required by the Minister, within fourteen days of the receipt by him of that additional information.

(2) When the Minister is of the opinion that it is in the public interest to do so, he may issue a licence under this Ordinance to the applicant upon payment of the prescribed fee.

Licence and conditions

15.(1) A licence issued under this Ordinance must show the kinds of off-shore banking to be done from within Nevis by the licensee.

(2) A licence under this Ordinance is subject to such conditions as the Minister may specify in respect of the offshore banking to be done by the licensee from within Nevis.

(3) A licence under this Ordinance remains valid until revoked pursuant this Ordinance but it is a condition of every licence that an annual fee be paid by every class of licensee in the amount and at the time prescribed.

(4) It is a condition of a licence under this Ordinance that the licensee will notify the Permanent Secretary of the creation by it of any subsidiary company within the meaning of section 13 and that it will notify the Permanent Secretary whenever it opens a place of business outside Nevis.

(5) Subsection (4) does not apply to a licensee that is a qualified foreign bank but the licensee shall not, without notifying the Permanent Secretary of its intention to do so, create any subsidiary company within the meaning of section 13 to carry on offshore banking from within Nevis.

Other special conditions

16. (1) It is a condition of a licence under this Ordinance that

(a) any voting shares of the licensee's capital will be in registered form;

(b) the licensee will not, without the approval of the Minister;

(i) enter into a merger, amalgamation or consolidation,

(ii) transfer, otherwise than in the ordinary course of its business, the whole or any substantial part of its assets or liabilities,

(iii) change its name from that set out in its licence,

(iv) alter its memorandum or articles of association, or

(v) transfer any of its shares;

(c) the licensee will not knowingly in the course of its business accept any deposit for the account of a resident of Nevis or keep a resident of Nevis as a customer for any of its offshore banking services, or

(d) the licensee that is a qualified foreign bank will, in the manner and to the extent prescribed, separate offshore banking activities from its other activities in Nevis and keep separate records of its offshore banking activities and will permit and assist in an audit of all its undertakings in Nevis by auditors approved by the Minister.

(2) Before giving an approval to any matter mentioned in subsection (1) the Minister shall carry out such of the investigations specified in section 13 as he thinks required.

(3) Paragraphs (a) and (b) of subsection (1) and subsection (2) do not apply to a licensee that is a qualified foreign bank.

Display of licence

17. A licensee shall display in a conspicuous place at each place where it does business a copy of its current licence under this Ordinance.

Revocation of licence

18.(1) The Minister may revoke a licence if the licensee

   (a) does not within six months after the issuance of its licence commence business;

   (b) fails to comply with a condition of its licence;

   (c) is in breach of any duty or obligation imposed upon it by this Ordinance or commits an offence under this Ordinance; or

   (d) ceases to carry on business under its licence.

(2) When the Minister intends to revoke a licence under subsection (1) it is his duty to give the licensee notice of his intention and a reasonable opportunity to show cause why the licence should not be revoked.

(3) The Minister must give notice in writing to the licensee of the revocation of the licence.

Right of appeal

19.(1) Any person who is aggrieved by the revocation of a licence by the Minister under section 18 may, within twenty-one days of the giving of the notice under section 18(3), appeal the revocation to a judge of the High Court, in chambers, whose decision thereon is final.

(2) Where the Minister revokes a licence and there is no appeal or where there is an appeal and the appeal is disallowed, the notice of the revocation must be published in the Gazette and in a newspaper of general circulation in Nevis.

Misleading name

20. No licensee may be granted a licence under a name of an existing bank trust company or other company carrying on business in Nevis or elsewhere as would in the opinion of the Minister mislead or confuse the persons for whom it intends to provide any or all of its services.

Service on licensee

21.(1) Before it does any offshore banking from within Nevis a licensee must deposit with the Permanent Secretary

>   *(a)* a duly executed instrument that appoints the Permanent Secretary as its agent for the acceptance of service of documents in any action arising out of the operations of the licensee; and

>   *(b)* a certificate setting out the name and address of any person in Nevis to whom documents related to the licensee and served on the Permanent Secretary are to be forwarded.

(2) It is the duty of the Permanent Secretary to ensure that all process, instruments and other documents served on him pursuant to subsection (1) in respect of a licensee are forwarded within ten days to the person named in a certificate described in paragraph (1) (b) in the case of that licensee.

Financial obligation

22.(1) A licence may be issued under this Ordinance to an eligible company when

> *(a)* the authorised capital of the company is at least two million dollars; and

> *(b)* capital to an amount of not less than one million dollars has been subscribed and paid-up in cash, such cash shall be deposited in an account maintained by the Permanent Secretary at the Eastern Caribbean Central Bank.

(2) For the purposes of this section and section 13, a licensee is controlled by another company or by an individual or government, if at the relevant time it is effectively controlled directly or indirectly by that other company, individual or government

> *(a)* through being an associate within the meaning of section 13 of that other company, individual or government;

> *(b)* through being an affiliate within the meaning of section 13 of that other company;

> *(c)* through the holding of shares of an incorporated body, but subject to subsection (4);

> *(d)* through the holding of membership in an unincorporated body;

> *(e)* through voting trusts or other agreements relating to the voting of shares;

> *(f)* through the holding by an unincorporated body of a substantial portion of the licensee's borrowings;

(g) through management control of an unincorporated body; or

(h) through any other similar means.

(4) A company is controlled by a person if shares of the company that carry voting rights sufficient to elect a majority of the directors of the company are held, directly, other than by way of security only, by or on behalf of that person.

(5) Whether or not any licensee is effectively controlled directly or indirectly by persons who are residents of Nevis is a question of fact determinable by the Minister whose decision thereon is final for the purposes of this Ordinance.

Reserves

23.(1) Subject to subsection (2), a licensee shall maintain a reserve fund and shall out of its net profits of each year and before any dividend is paid transfer to the fund a sum equal to not less than twenty-five per cent of those profits whenever the amount of the reserve fund is less than the paid-up capital of the licensee.

(2) Subsection (1) does not apply to a licensee for whom it is shown to the satisfaction of the Minister that the aggregate reserves of the licensee are adequate in relation to its business.

Dividends

24. A licensee shall not declare or pay a dividend if there are reasonable grounds for believing that

(a) the licensee is, or would after the payment be, unable to pay its liabilities as they become due, or

(b) the realizable value of the licensee's assets would thereby be less than the aggregate of its liabilities and capital.

Part III - Abandoned Property

Abandoned property

25.(1) Property of the following kinds held or owing in the course of its business by a licensee in respect of which no activity has been evidenced for a period of ten years is abandoned property:

> *(a)* any general deposit, that is a demand saving or matured time deposit made with the licensee together with any interest or dividends but exclusive of legal charges;

> *(b)* funds that were paid towards the purchase of shares or other interests in a licensee;

> *(c)* any sum payable on cheques or other instruments on which the licensee is liable; and in respect of which the licensee has, by registered mail to the latest known address of the lessee, given notice of its intention to deliver the contents into the custody of the Nevis Island Administration and the lessee has failed to respond within a period of one year.

(2) Activity is evidenced in respect of the property described in subsection (1) if the owner thereof has

> *(a)* within ten years of the date of deposit increased or decreased the amount of the deposit or presented a passbook or other record for the crediting of interest in respect of the deposit;

> *(b)* within ten years of paying funds for the purchase of shares or other interest mentioned in subsection (1)(b), increased or decreased the amount of the funds or presented a document or book for crediting of dividends in respect thereof;

(c) within ten years of making the last deposit, inquiry or communication concerning any item mentioned in subsection (1), corresponded with the licensee concerning the items or otherwise indicated an interest in the items as evidenced by a memorandum about them by the licensee.

Disposal of abandoned property

26.(1) A licensee shall, once in each financial year, report to the Permanent Secretary all its holding of abandoned property within the meaning of this Ordinance and shall, from time to time, deposit with or convey to the Nevis Island Administration in the prescribed manner all abandoned property.

(2) When a licensee has deposited with or conveyed to the Nevis Island Administration any abandoned property, the licensee is relieved from any liability to the beneficial owners thereof to the extent of the value of the property deposited or conveyed to the Nevis Island Administration.

(3) Within thirty days after reporting to the Permanent Secretary pursuant to subsection (1), the Permanent Secretary shall give notice by registered mail to the beneficial owner of the property, at his latest known address; but with the approval of the High Court on application thereto, the Permanent Secretary may be exempted from mailing the copy of the notice to the owner.

Sale of abandoned property

27.(1) The Nevis Island Administration may sell at public auction any property that has been conveyed to it under section 26 after the expiration of thirty days from the latest of the date of publication of the notice referred to in section 26(3) and the mailing of the copy of the notice to the owner, as the case may be.

(2) The public auction may be held after such reasonable advertising of the sale as the Nevis Island Administration considers suitable.

Payment to Consolidated Fund

28. The Permanent Secretary shall pay into the Nevis Island Consolidated Fund all money received by the Nevis Island Administration as abandoned property and the proceeds of the public auction of any abandoned property less, in each case

(a) such amount as the Minister considers necessary to reserve for the payment of claims later made and approved by him; and

(b) amounts deducted by the Permanent Secretary as approved by the Minister for reasonable expenses incurred in connection with the publishing and mailing of notice, service charges, and the sale of abandoned property.

Claims against property

29.(1) A person who claims a beneficial interest in any abandoned property deposited with or conveyed to the Nevis Island Administration may make a claim for the value thereof within the prescribed time and in the prescribed manner.

(2) When the Minister is satisfied that a claimant is entitled to the abandoned property, the Nevis Island Administration shall deliver up the property, or make payment for the value thereof, as the case requires.

Notice to claimants

30.(1) When the Minister admits or refuses a claim under section 29, he shall forthwith notify the claimants of his decision.

(2) A person aggrieved by a refusal of his claim for abandoned property by the Minister may within twenty-one days of receiving notice of the refusal, appeal the decision to a judge of the High Court in chambers who may make such order thereon as he considers equitable.

Offence re abandoned property

31. A licensee that fails to report to the Permanent Secretary any abandoned property in its possession or that fails to deposit with or convey to the Nevis Island Administration any abandoned property as required by this Ordinance, is guilty of an offence and liable on summary conviction to a fine not exceeding twenty five thousand dollars.

Part IV - Administration Of Licensees

Director

32. For the purpose of this Ordinance,

(a) "**director**" means an individual occupying the like position and performing the like functions of a director under the Companies Act, however his position is designated.

(b) a reference to "**directors**" refers to the board of directors or the body directing the affairs of a company or firm.

Office of director

33. A director of a licensee cease to hold office as a director thereof

(a) if he becomes bankrupt or suspends payment to his creditors;

(b) if he is convicted in Nevis of an offence triable on indictment; or

(c) if he is convicted outside Nevis of an offence that would be triable on indictment had it been committed in Nevis;

(d) if he becomes of unsound mind.

Disqualification of director

34. A person who has been a director of a licensee whose licence is revoked under this Ordinance shall not, without the prior approval of the Minister act or continue to act as a director of any other licensee.

Disclosure of interest

35.(1) A director of a licensee who is interested, directly or indirectly in an advance or loan from the licensee shall as soon as possible declare the nature of his interest to its directors at a meeting thereof.

(2) Subsection (1) does not apply when the interest of a director in an advance or loan consists only of being a creditor of or having an interest in a firm that is interested in an advance or loan from the licensee if, in either case, the interest of the director is not a substantial interest.

(3) A declaration by a director of a licensee that he is interested in any advance or loan that may, after the date of the declaration, be made by the licensee is a sufficient declaration of interest in relation to any advance or loan made after the declaration, if

(a) the declaration specified the nature and extent of the interest; and

(b) the interest of the director is not different in nature from, or greater than, the nature and extent so specified in the declaration at the time any advance or loan is made.

Declaration of interest

36.(1) A director of a licensee who holds any office or has any interest in any property whereby, directly or indirectly, his functions under this Ordinance are likely to be in conflict with his personal interests shall declare the nature, character and extent of that office or interest to the directors at a meeting thereof.

(2) A declaration required under this section shall be made *(a)* at the first meeting of the directors that is held after the acquisition by the declarant of that relevant office or interest, or

(b) if the declarant was not at that time a director, after he becomes a director.

(3) A director to whom this section or section 35 applies shall in any event notify the Secretary of the licensee of his interest so that the Secretary may convene a meeting of the Board of Directors for the purpose of considering the declaration, unless a meeting of the Board of Directors is already scheduled to be held within 14 days following the receipt of notification by the Secretary of the Director's declaration.

Recording declaration

37. A director of a licensee who has declared any interest referred to in section 35 or 36 shall

(a) cause the declaration made by him thereunder to be brought up and read at the next meeting of the directors after it was given; and

(b) cause the declaration to be recorded in the minutes of the meeting at which it was made or read or both.

Offence

38. A director of a licensee who contravenes section 34, 35 or 36 is guilty of an offence and liable on conviction to a fine not exceeding five thousand dollars or to imprisonment for twelve months or to both.

Insider information

39.(1) A person who has acquired confidential information concerning a licensee

(a) as a director, officer, employee or auditor of the licensee,

(b) as a custodian of the licensee, or

(c) as an employee of the Nevis Island Administration shall not disclose that information to any person except as permitted under subsection (2) or use that information for any personal benefit not related to the duties through which the information was acquired.

(2) Subsection (1) does not apply to the giving of confidential information

(a) when the information is a general credit rating of a person that is supplied by a director, officer or employee of the licensee following a bona fide business request;

(b) when the information is given with the written authorization of the beneficiary or his legal representative;

(c) when the information is lawfully required to be disclosed by an order of the High Court, or

(d) when the information is lawfully disclosed pursuant to any other enactment.

(4) In this section **"confidential information"** means information concerning the identity of a depositor or concerning the assets, liabilities, transactions or other information in respect of a depositor.

Part V - Audit And Inspection

Financial Statements

40.(1) A licensee shall, in respect of its business, submit to the Permanent Secretary in prescribed form

> *(a)* not later than twenty-one days after the end of each three month period, a quarterly statement of the assets and liabilities of the licensee; and

> *(b)* within such time as the Minister may determine, such other returns as the Permanent Secretary requires

(2) The Minister may require a licensee to submit such further information as he considers necessary for the proper understanding of any statement or return furnished by the licensee pursuant to subsection (1) and the further information shall be submitted within such time and in such manner as the Minister requires.

Confidentiality

41.(1) No statement, return or information shall be required by the Permanent Secretary or the Minister with respect to the affairs of any particular offshore banking customer of a licensee, but the Minister may seek and be informed of the names of any residents of Nevis who are customers of the licensee.

(2) No statement, returns or information furnished or submitted by a licensee in respect of its business shall be communicated or disclosed except to the Minister and such public officers and other persons as may be prescribed.

Publication of balance sheets

42.(1) Not later than four months after the close of its financial year or such longer period as the Minister may allow, a licensee shall forward to the Permanent Secretary copies of its balance sheet and profit and loss account and the full and correct names of the directors of the licensee.

(2) The balance sheet and the profit and loss account must bear on its face the certificate of an auditor.

Auditor

43. In this Ordinance, unless the context otherwise requires-

"**auditor**" means a person who

(a) is qualified as an accountant by examination of, one of the institutes of Chartered Accountants or Certified Accountants in England and Wales, Ireland or Scotland, the Canadian Institute of Chartered Accountants or the American Institute of Certified Public Accountants and holds a current practising certificate if required by his institute to do so; or

(b) possesses such other qualification in accountancy, banking or other similar qualification equivalent to the qualification set forth in paragraph (a) as the Minister may, by order, approve and is in good standing with respect to such qualification.

Annual auditing

44.(1) The annual balance sheets, and accounts of a licensee shall be audited at least once in every financial year by an auditor appointed by the licensee from a list of auditors maintained by the Permanent Secretary.

(2) It is the duty of the auditor appointed pursuant to subsection (1) to submit a report to the shareholders of the licensee and to the Permanent Secretary.

(3) The report of the auditor shall state whether the auditor has obtained all the information and explanations he needed and in addition state whether in his opinion the balance sheet and accounts exhibit a true and correct view of the assets and liabilities of the licensee as at the date of the statement, and the income and expenditure of the licensee for the year then ended.

(4) It is the duty of the auditor to note in his report any instances where the operations of the licensee might not in the opinion of the auditor be in compliance with the requirements of this Ordinance or any regulations made hereunder, the conditions of the licensee's licence or its memorandum or articles of association.

(5) The report of the auditor shall be read with the report of the directors to the shareholders at the annual meeting of the licensee.

(6) A copy of the report of the auditor shall be displayed by the licensee in a conspicuous place at its office in Nevis.

(7) If the Permanent Secretary has reasonable grounds for not being satisfied with the annual report of an auditor appointed by a licensee, the Permanent Secretary may appoint another auditor to make an independent report.

(8) When a licensee fails to appoint an auditor pursuant to this section, the Permanent Secretary may appoint an auditor who has all the powers of an auditor appointed by the licensee to carry out an audit.

(9) The remuneration of an auditor shall be paid by the licensee to which he is appointed and, if the auditor is appointed under subsection (7) or (8), his remuneration shall be such amount as the Minister determines.

Prohibited auditors

45. No person may be appointed an auditor of a licensee

(a) if he has any proprietary interest in the licensee,

(b) if he is a director, or agent of the licensee or of an affiliate of the licensee, within the meaning of section 13; or

(c) if he is an officer or employee of the Nevis Island Administration.

Examination by Minister

46.(1) When the Minister has reasonable grounds to believe that a licensee is not in a sound financial condition or that it is not acting in compliance with this Ordinance, the Minister may apply to the High Court for an order to examine the affairs of the licensee.

(2) The High Court may, having regard to the purposes of this Ordinance, grant an application under subsection (1) subject to such conditions as the High Court considers appropriate in all the circumstances.

(3) When the High Court grants an application under subsection (2) the Minister shall appoint a fit and proper person to examine the licensee.

Powers of examiners

47.(1) Subject to subsection (2), a licensee shall produce for an examiner appointed under section 46 by the Minister at such time as the examiner fixes, all books, minutes, cash, securities, vouchers and other documents and records relating to its assets, liabilities and business generally and shall give the examiner such information concerning its affairs and business as he may request.

(2) An examiner may not have access to, nor shall he be given access to, the name or theaccount of any depositor if the depositor is not a resident of Nevis.

Access by court order

48. Notwithstanding section 47 (2), the High Court may, on the application of the Minister, order the production of information protected under that section if the court is satisfied that it is required in the public interest by the examiner for the proper performance of his functions under this Ordinance and that there are no other lawful means of acquiring the information.

Offence and penalty

49. If any of the matters referred to in section 47 are not produced, or the information relating thereto is not given, to the examiner by the licensee, the licensee is guilty of an offence and liable on summary conviction to a fine of five thousand dollars and in addition, to a further fine of five hundred dollars for each day during which the offence continues.

Remedial action

50.(1) When the Minister is of the opinion that an examination of a licensee indicates that the licensee is carrying on its business in an unlawful manner or is an unsound financial condition, the Minister may

> *(a)* require that the licensee immediately take such remedial measures as he considers necessary; and

(b) appoint a person who in his opinion has had training and experience in the business of the licensee concerned, to advise the licensee on the action to be taken to remedy the situation, or

(c) suspend the licence of the licensee for a period not exceeding three months.

(2) A person appointed under subsection (1)(b) shall be paid by the Nevis Island Administration such remuneration as the Minister may determine, which remunerationshall be charged to the licensee concerned.

Part VI - Offences

Unlicensed offshore banking

51.(1) A person who does offshore banking from within Nevis during any period in which he does not hold a licence under this Ordinance is guilty of an offence and liable on conviction to a fine not exceeding two hundred and fifty thousand dollars.

(2) Any director or officer of a company that does offshore banking from within Nevis without a licence under this Ordinance is guilty of an offence and liable on conviction to a fine not exceeding fifty thousand dollars or to imprisonment for five years or to both such fine and imprisonment.

(3) Subject to subsection 4 a person who holds any funds obtained from doing offshore banking business from within Nevis during any period in which he did not hold a licence under this Ordinance shall repay those funds in accordance with the direction of the Minister.

(4) The High Court may order any profits derived from the conduct of offshore banking from within Nevis without a licence under this Ordinance to be forfeited to the Nevis Island Administration.

Misleading advertising

52.(1) A licensee that engages in advertising practices that are likely to mislead concerning

> *(a)* the relationship of the licensee with the Nevis Island Administration or any department or office thereof;

> *(b)* the true interest rate paid on deposit or charged or credit;

> *(c)* the true returns on the management of investments;

(d) the insured or guaranteed status of deposit or other liabilities or of investments managed by it; or

(e) the financial condition of the designated institution; is guilty of an offence and liable on conviction to a fine not exceeding ten thousand dollars.

(2) A licensee shall, in respect of its business, furnish the Permanent Secretary with copies of all its advertisements.

False statement and obstruction

53. A director, officer, employee or agent of a licensee, who, with intent to deceive,

(a) makes any false or misleading statement or entry in a book, account, record, report or statement of the licensee or omits a statement or entry that should be made therein, or

(b) obstructs

(i) the carrying out by an auditor of his proper function under this Ordinance, or

(ii) the examination of a licensee as required pursuant to this Ordinance is guilty of an offence and liable on summary conviction to a fine not exceeding fifty thousand dollars or imprisonment for five years or to both.

Disclosure of confidential information

54. A person referred to in section 39(1) who discloses confidential information contrary to that section is guilty of an offence and liable on conviction to a fine not exceeding twenty thousand dollars or to imprisonment for twelve months or both.

Contravention of section 42

55. A licensee that contravenes section 42 is guilty of an offence and liable on conviction to a fine not exceeding twenty thousand dollars and in addition to a further fine of one thousand dollars for each month during which the offence continues after a conviction is obtained.

Part VII - General

Extending time

56. At the request of a licensee, the Minister may extend the time within which any document or information required from the licensee under this Ordinance must be sent to the Permanent Secretary.

Regulations

57. The Minister may make such regulations as are necessary for the purpose of this Ordinance and, in particular, may make regulations in respect of such acts, matters or things as are required by this Ordinance to be prescribed.

Use of "bank" in names

58.(1) Subject to subsection (2) no person other than a licensee may, without the approval of the Minister use the word

(a) "**bank**" or any of its derivatives in any language, or

(b) any other word indicating the doing of offshore banking from within Nevis, in the name, description or title under which that person carries on business or intends to carry on business in Nevis or make any representation to that effect in any bill head, letter paper, notice or advertisement.

(2) Subsection (1) does not apply

(a) to a bank licensed under the Banking Act;

(b) to a qualified foreign bank or eligible company that is applying for a licence under this Ordinance as a licensee;

(3) A person who contravenes subsection (1) is guilty of an offence and liable on conviction to a fine not exceeding twenty thousand dollars.

Part VIII - Winding-up

Voluntary winding-up

59.(1) Except with the prior written approval of the Minister no licensee may be wound-up voluntarily.

(2) Approval for a voluntary winding-up of a licensee may be given by the Minister only if he is satisfied that

(a) the licensee is solvent and has sufficient assets to repay it depositors and other creditors without delay; and

(b) subject to subsection (3), the winding-up has been approved by the holders of at least two-thirds of the outstanding voting shares of the licensee.

(3) Where the Minister finds in respect of a licensee that there is imminent danger of its insolvency, the Minister may waive the requirement for shareholder approval of the winding-up of the licensee voluntarily, if

(a) the winding-up is to be effected in whole or in part through the sale of any of the assets of the licensee to another licensee; and

(b) the deposit liabilities of the licensee to be wound-up are to be assumed by that other licensee.

Commencement of voluntary winding-up

60. When a licensee receives the approval of the Minister to its voluntary winding-up, the licensee shall

(a) cease to do business immediately and retain only such staff as is necessary for an orderly winding-up;

(b) repay its depositors and other creditors; and

(c) wind-up all operations undertaken before the receipt of the approval to wind-up.

Notice of winding-up

61.(1) Within thirty days of the receipt of the approval of the Minister to the winding-up a notice of voluntary winding-up which must contain the prescribed information, shall be sent by the licensee in the prescribed manner or by personal service, to the depositors and creditors of the licensee and other persons having any interest in its funds or other property.

(2) The notice described in subsection (1) shall also be published in the Gazette and placed in a conspicuous place on the premises of each office or branch of the licensee to be wound-up.

Settlement of claims

62.(1) The approval of the Minister to the voluntary winding-up of a licensee does not adversely affect the rights of a depositor or other creditor of the licensee to settlement in full of his claim nor the rights of any person having an interest in the funds or property of the licensee to settlement of that interest.

(2) All claims made by persons described in subsection (1) shall be settled by the licensee concerned within such time as the Minister may determine.

Distribution of remaining assets

63.(1) The assets of a licensee being voluntarily wound-up that remain after settlement of the claims described in section 62 are to be distributed among the shareholders of the licensee in proportion to their respective rights.

(2) Notwithstanding subsection (1) , no distribution of the remaining assets of a licensee may be made

(a) before all claims of depositors and other creditors have been settled or, in the case of a disputed claim, before the licensee has deposited with the Nevis Island Administration sufficient funds to meet any liability that could arise under that claim;

(b) before any funds that are payable to a depositor or other creditor who has made his claim have been deposited with the Nevis Island Administration; or

(c) before any funds or property held by the licensee that could not be returned, in accordance with section 62, to the persons who have an interest therein have been deposited with or transferred to the Nevis Island Administration, together with the relevant records.

Interruption of winding-up

64.(1) If the Minister determines that the assets of a licensee that is being voluntarily wound-up are not sufficient for the full discharge of the obligations of the licensee or that the completion of such a winding-up is being unduly delayed, the Minister may seize the management and control of the licensee by posting a notice to that effect on the premises of the licensee and by putting persons appointed by the Minister into the offices of the licensee.

(2) When the Minister seizes the management and control of a licensee under subsection (1) he shall immediately begin proceedings for the compulsory winding-up of the licensee or its re-organisation, in accordance with this Ordinance.

Seizure in other cases

65.(1) Notwithstanding section 64, the Minister may seize the management and control of a licensee in any of the following circumstances, namely

(a) when the realizable value of the licensee's assets is less than the aggregate of its liabilities and capital accounts or the licensee's financial condition suggests that it will shortly be in that circumstance;

(b) when its business is being conducted in an imprudent manner or is not being conducted in accordance with this Ordinance;

(c) when the licensee refuses to submit to inspection of its records or operations by an auditor appointed under section 44 or an examiner appointed under section 46; or

(d) when its licence has been revoked or suspended under this Ordinance.

(2) A seizure of the management and control of a licensee under this section is effected by placing a notice to that effect on the premises of the licensee and by putting persons appointed by the Minister into the offices of the licensee.

(3) A licensee aggrieved by a seizure under this section may institute proceedings in the High Court for recovery of the administration and control of the institution and the High Court may make such order in respect thereto as to it seems just and consistent with the purposes of this Ordinance.

Duty of Minister

66. Within thirty days after the Minister has seized the administration and control of a licensee under this Ordinance, the Minister shall begin proceedings in the High Court

(a) for the compulsory winding-up of the licensee; or

(b) for the reorganisation of the licensee.

Power of High Court

67. The High Court may in respect of proceedings by the Minister under section 66 order

(a) the compulsory winding-up of the licensee;

(b) the reorganisation of the licensee subject to such terms and conditions as the court may determine; or

(c) the return of the management and control of the licensee to its shareholders, directors and officers subject to such safeguards or conditions, if any, as the court may consider for the purposes of this Ordinance.

Notice of application

68.(1) Forthwith after he makes an application to the High Court under section 66 in relation to a licensee, the Minister shall give notice of the application

(a) to the directors and shareholders of the licensee, and

(b) to the depositors and other creditors of the licensee.

Appointment of custodian

69. If the High Court orders the compulsory winding-up or reorganisation of a licensee pursuant to an application under section 67, the High Court shall appoint a custodian to be responsible to the Court and to supervise the winding-up or re-organisation of the licensee.

Functions of custodian

70.(1) In respect of the licensee for which he has been appointed, the custodian has the exclusive power and duty to manage and control the affairs of the licensee.

(2) Without limiting his powers or duties under subsection (1), the custodian may, in respect of the licensee for which he has been appointed,

> *(a)* continue or discontinue its operations;

> *(b)* stop or limit the payment of its obligations;

> *(c)* employ staff;

> *(d)* execute any instrument in its name;

> *(e)* initiate, defend and conduct in its name any action or proceeding to which the licensee is or might be a party;

> *(f)* end the seizure of the licensee by restoring it to its directors and shareholders; and

> *(g)* re-organise or wind-up the licensee in accordance with this Ordinance.

Inventory of assets

71.(1) Forthwith after assuming management and control of a licensee, the custodian shall make an inventory of its assets and forward a copy of the inventory to the Registrar of the High Court.

(2) The copy of the inventory forwarded to the Registrar shall be kept available at all reasonable times for the inspection of interested persons.

Reorganisation

72.(1) Where the re-organisation of a licensee has been ordered by the High Court, the custodian shall develop a plan of re-organisation and deliver a copy thereof to each of the depositors and other creditors of the licensee who under the plan would not receive full restitution or payment of their claims.

(2) The copy of the re-organisation plan must be accompanied by a notice requiring that objections to the plan be delivered to the custodian not later than thirty days after the last of the copies have been delivered under subsection (1).

(3) If within the time limited therefor by subsection (2) the custodian does not receive objections in writing to the re-organisation from persons who in the aggregate hold at least one-third of the total amount of deposits and other liabilities of the licensee, the custodian may carry out the re-organisation plan referred to in subsection (1).

(4) When an objection to the re-organisation plan is received from one-third or more of the persons described in subsection (3), the custodian shall submit further re-organisation plans in like manner until such time as fewer than one-third of the persons described in subsection (3) object within the time limited therefor or he may refer the matter back, at anytime to the High Court for further directions.

(5) The High Court may extend the time limited by subsection (1) and upon cause shown may exempt the custodian from delivering the plan to some or all of the persons mentioned in subsection (1).

Content of plan

73. A re-organisation plan developed by the custodian of a licensee must, so far as it is practicable to do so (*a*) be equitable to all classes of depositors;

(*b*) provide for bringing in new funds to establish adequate ratios between

(**i**) capital and deposits, and

(**ii**) liquid assets and deposits; and

(*c*) provide for the removal of any directors or any officer or employee responsible for the circumstances that led to the seizure of the licensee.

Application for order by custodian

74. If, in the course of the re-organisation of a licensee, it appears to the custodian that circumstances render the plan or its execution undesirable, he may apply to the High Court for an order

(*a*) to modify the plan, or

(*b*) to wind-up the licensee compulsorily.

Compulsory winding-up

75.(1) Where the High Court under section 67 or 74 orders the compulsory winding-up of a licensee, the custodian appointed therefor by the Court may, subject to subsection (2), perform the functions of the licensee.

(2) The custodian of a licensee described in subsection (1) may not, without an order of the High Court to do so,

(*a*) sell any assets or transfer any property of the licensee that has a value exceeding one hundred thousand dollars;

(b) create a security interest in any asset or property of the licensee in favour of a creditor who extends a new credit to the licensee;

(c) compromise or release any claim the amount of which exceeds one hundred thousand dollars; or

(d) pay any claim other than one in respect of an obligation incurred by the custodian in the exercise of his winding-up functions before the schedule referred to in section 79(c) has been approved by the High Court.

Termination of service contracts

76. Subject to any other law governing conditions of employment, the custodian of a licensee that has been ordered by the High Court to be compulsorily wound-up shall terminate not later than nine months after the order of the High Court

(a) any employment contract of the licensee;

(b) any contract for services which the licensee is a party, and

(c) any obligations of the licensee as a lessee of property.

Right of lessor

77. A lessor of any property referred to in section 76

(a) must be given notice of not less than ninety days of the intended termination of the obligations of a licensee thereunder;

(b) has no claim for rent thereunder other than rent accrued on the date of the termination of the obligation of the licensee; and

(c) has no right to damages by reason only of any termination of the obligations of the licensee, notwithstanding any term of the lease to the contrary.

Statements of accounts

78.(1) Within sixty days after an order for the compulsory winding-up of a licensee, the custodian shall deliver a statement of account to any depositors and other creditors.

(2) The statement of account is a statement of the nature and amount for which a claim of a person described in subsection (1) is shown on the books of the licensee.

(3) A notice specifying that any objection to the statement of account is to be made on a date specified in the notice, not being later than sixty days after the delivery of the notice, must accompany the statement of account.

(4) The High Court on application of the custodian for cause shown may exempt the custodian from delivering a statement of account to any person mentioned in subsection (1).

Claims

79. Not later than ninety days after the last day specified in the notice for filing claims against a licensee being compulsorily wound-up, the custodian shall

(a) reject any claim, of which he doubts the validity;

(b) determine the amount, if any, owing to each known depositor or other creditor and the priority of his claim under this Ordinance;

(c) prepare for filing with the High Court a schedule of the actions proposed to be undertaken for the purpose of the compulsory winding-up of the licensee;

(d) notify each person whose claim is allowed in full; and

(e) publish, once a week for three consecutive weeks in a newspaper of general circulation in Nevis,

> **(i)** a notice of the date and place where the schedule referred to in paragraph (c) will be available for inspection, and

> **(ii)** the date, not being earlier than thirty days from the date of the publication, on which the custodian will file that schedule with the High Court.

Objections

80.(1) Within twenty days of the filing of a schedule under section 79, a depositor or other creditor or shareholder of the licensee concerned, or other interested person, may file with the High Court any objection he has to any action proposed in the schedule referred to in section 79(c).

(2) After notice served on the custodian and such interested parties as the High Court may require, the High Court shall hear the objection and make such order thereon as it considers just in the circumstances.

(3) When the High Court allows an objection, the order must set out the manner in which the schedule referred to in section 79(c) is to be modified.

Distribution of assets

81.(1) When a schedule has been filed under section 79 in respect of a licensee, the custodian may make a partial distribution to the claimants against the licensee whose claims are undisputed or allowed by the High Court, if the custodian establishes an adequate reserve for the payment of disputed claims against the licensee.

(2) As soon as practicable after all objections against the distribution proposed by the custodian have been heard and determined, final distribution of the assets of the licensee concerned shall be made by the custodian.

Priority of claims

82.(1) The following claims have priority against the general assets of a licensee being compulsorily wound-up under this Ordinance

(a) firstly, the necessary and reasonable expenses incurred by the custodian in carrying out his functions under this Ordinance;

(b) secondly, the wages and salaries of the officers and employees of the licensee that accrued during the three months immediately preceding the seizure of the licensee under this Ordinance;

(c) thirdly, any monies owing to the Nevis Island Administration;

(d) fourthly, the other deposits.

(2) After payment of all other claims against the licensee, with interest at such rate as the High Court determines, all remaining claims against the licensee that were not filed within the time limited therefor under this Ordinance may then be paid.

(3) Where the amount available to pay the claims of any class of claimant specified in this section in respect of priorities is not sufficient to provide payment in full to claimants in that class, the amount available shall be distributed by the custodian on a pro rata basis among the claimants in that class.

Distribution to shareholders

83. The assets of a licensee being compulsorily wound-up that remain after the final distribution to claimants pursuant to section 82 shall be distributed by the custodian among the shareholders of the licensee in proportion to their respective rights.

Abandoned funds

84.(1) Any funds of a licensee being compulsorily wound-up under this Ordinance that remain unclaimed after the final distribution under section 82 and not subject to distribution under any other provision of this Ordinance shall be deposited with the Nevis Island Administration by the custodian of the licensee.

(2) Funds deposited with it under subsection (1) must be held by the Nevis Island Administration for ten years unless earlier claimed by a person entitled thereto.

(3) On the expiration of the ten years referred to in subsection (1) in respect of any funds, those funds remaining unclaimed become abandoned property.

Completion of winding-up

85.(1) When all the assets of a licensee being wound-up have been distributed or dealt with as required by this Ordinance, the custodian shall render an audited statement to the High Court.

(2) If the High Court is satisfied with the audited statement rendered by the custodian in respect of a licensee being wound-up, it may by order direct the Registrar of the companies to strike the name of the licensee from the register of companies under the Companies Act and publish notice thereof in the Gazette.

(3) When its name is struck off the register of companies the licensee is thereupon dissolved and its licence under this Ordinance is revoked.

Part IX - Residence

Residents of Nevis

86.(1) For the purposes of this Ordinance, the following are residents of Nevis, namely:

> *(a)* an individual ordinarily resident in Nevis or a citizen of St. Kitts and Nevis with a residence in Nevis;
>
> *(b)* any incorporated or other body, incorporated, formed or organised in Nevis the majority of the shares or other ownership of which is not beneficially held by persons resident outside Nevis;
>
> *(c)* any incorporated or other body, wherever incorporated, formed or organised, that is controlled within the meaning of section 22 by a person described in paragraph (a) or (b);
>
> *(d)* any incorporated body or other body that is controlled within the meaning of section 22 by a body described in paragraph (c) or by the Nevis Island Administration or any agency thereof;

(2) A reference in this Part to any beneficial interest, or to any thing being beneficially owned or held includes ownership through a trustee, legal representative, agent or other intermediary.

Persons resident outside Nevis

87. A person is resident outside Nevis for the purpose of this Ordinance if he is not a resident of Nevis within the meaning of section 86.

Part X - Tax Exemptions

Exemption from tax

88.(1) Except as provided by this Part, no income tax, capital gains tax or other direct tax shall be levied in Nevis upon the profits or gains of a licensee in respect of the offshore banking it does from within Nevis.

(2) Except as provided by this Part, no income tax, capital gains tax or other direct tax shall be levied in Nevis in respect of any dividends or earnings attributable to the shares or securities of a licensee that are beneficially owned by another licensee or by a person who is not a resident of Nevis.

(3) Except as provided by this Part, no estate, inheritance, succession or similar tax shall be levied in Nevis in respect of any shares, securities or assets of a licensee that are beneficially owned by a person who is not a resident of Nevis.

(4) Except as provided by this Part, no tax or duty shall be levied upon the increment in value of the property or other assets in Nevis of a licensee other than upon such of them as are distributed to residents of Nevis.

Transfer of assets exemption

89.(1) Except as provided by this Part, no tax or duty shall be levied upon a licensee, its shareholders or transferees in respect of the transfer of all or any part of its securities or other assets to another licensee or to a person who is not a resident of Nevis.

(2) Where a person who is not a resident of Nevis or a licensee transfers shares of a licensee that are held by that person or licensee to another person who is not a resident of Nevis or to another licensee, the transfer is exempt from the payment of any tax or duty thereon.

(3) Except as provided by this Part,

(a) no income tax or capital gains tax, and

(b) no other direct tax shall be levied or collected in Nevis in respect of any dividend, interest or other return from any shares, securities, deposits or other borrowing of a licensee or any assets managed by the licensee if the dividend, interest or other returns are in respect of shares, securities deposits or other borrowings or assets beneficially owned by a person who is not a resident of Nevis; but the onus of establishing ownership lies upon the licensee

Withholding tax and report re dividends etc.

90.(1) Notwithstanding any provision of the Income Tax Act, but subject to subsection (2), no licensee need withhold any portion of any dividend, interest or other returns payable to any person in respect of any borrowings of the licensee or in respect of that person holding shares or securities of the licensee.

(2) All dividends, interest or other returns attributable to the shares or securities of or the management of assets by a licensee that are payable to a resident of Nevis and known as such by the licensee shall be reported to the Inland Revenue Department.

Tax on profits

91.(1) By way of income tax but in lieu of income tax at the rates in the Income Tax Act, there shall be levied and paid to the Inland Revenue Department upon the profits and gains of a licensee, in respect of the offshore banking business done by it from within Nevis, tax at the following rates

(a) 2½% on all profits and gains up to ten million dollars;

(b) 2% on all profits and gains in amounts exceeding ten million dollars but not exceeding twenty million dollars;

(c) 1½% on all profits and gains in amounts exceeding twenty million dollars but not exceeding thirty million dollars; and

(d) 1% on all profits and gains in amounts exceeding thirty million dollars.

(2) Except in so far as this Ordinance operates to exempt a licensee from liability to income tax under the Income Tax Act, the provisions of that Act apply *mutatis mutandis* to a licensee.

Tax agreement

92.(1) Notwithstanding section 91, a licensee and the Minister may enter into an agreement determining the amount to be paid as income tax in lieu of other taxes on income by the licensee in respect of the business it does from within Nevis.

(2) An agreement under subsection (1) may not provide for any amount in lieu of other taxes if it would result in the licensee paying less than it would if it were to pay tax pursuant to section 91.

Service Fees etc.

93.(1) When a tax levied in Nevis is in the nature of a service charge or utility charge for a service provided by the Nevis Island Administration, a licensee is not exempt from that charge under this Part.

(2) A service or utility charge includes a charge or fee levied or imposed for the issuance of any incorporation, registration or licence required in Nevis.

Customs duty

94. The Minister may by order exempt a licensee in respect of its business from all or so much of any duty payable under the Customs Act in respect of any goods imported by the licensee in respect of its business as the Minister deems expedient, if the licensee in respect of its business satisfies the Minister that the goods concerned are not being made or manufactured in Nevis, are essential as equipment or fixtures for doing business from within Nevis and are not merely goods that will be used up or expended in the ordinary course of business.

Employee benefits

95.(1) Where the Minister is satisfied that a licensee must use the services of specially qualified persons in order to do its business effectively from within Nevis and that

> *(a)* it is unable to acquire those services in Nevis, and

> *(b)* it is unable to retain or hire those services from outside Nevis without special tax benefits being made available the Minister may authorise an offshore benefit provision for the employment of those specially qualified persons.

(2) An offshore benefit provisions is one whereby a prescribed percentage of an employee's or contractor's salary or fees from a licensee

> *(a)* is exempt from any duty or tax in Nevis;

> *(b)* may be paid in a foreign currency;

(c) may be paid in some other prescribed manner in another currency or otherwise; notwithstanding the provision of any other law to the contrary.

Part XI - Miscellaneous and Consequential Application of Companies Act

96.(1) The provisions of the Companies Act relating to the winding-up of a company do not apply to a licensee.

Bankruptcy Act

97. The Bankruptcy Act does not apply to a licensee.

Banking Act

98. The Banking Act does not apply to a licensee in respect of its offshore banking business.

Exemptions

99. The provisions of this Ordinance set out hereunder do not apply to a licensee that is a qualified foreign bank, namely:

  (a) sections 20 to 24;

  (b) sections 33 to 37;

  (c) Part VIII.

Commencement

100. This Ordinance comes into operation on a day to be fixed by the Minister.

A Source of Professional Help in Nevis

The First Nevisian Group provides offshore company and trust services, and a complete stockbrokerage service.

First Nevisian Stockbrokers Ltd. is authorized by the Nevis government to conduct stockbroking and investment business. Services offered include: Trading Equities on all Major and most Minor International Stock Markets, Trading International Fixed Interest Securities from U.S. Treasuries to Eurobonds, Trading all Major and most Minor Currencies, Trading Emerging Market Sovereign and Commercial Debt, Portfolio & Investment Management - Executionary, Advisory or Discretionary, Global Safe Custody Facilities, Client's accounts maintained in all major and most minor currencies.

For more information contact:
> First Nevisian Stockbrokers
> Attn: New Client Department
> Henville Building
> Prince Charles St.
> Charlestown
> Nevis
> West Indies
> Fax: (1) 869 469 1204

Please mark initial fax: Attn: New Client Department

First Nevisian Corporate Services Ltd. is a Registered Agent under the authority of the Nevis Island Government, specialising in the formation and administration of international corporate structures and trust structures. Services offered include: International Offshore Corporate Structures, Multi-National Trust & Company Formations, Offshore Bank Formations, Corporate & Trust - Administration and Management, Programs of Offshore Asset Protection, Offshore Private Banking Facilities, Issuance of Offshore Credit Cards

For more information contact:

        First Nevisian Corporate Services
        Attn: New Client Department
        Henville Building
        Prince Charles St.
        Charlestown
        Nevis
        West Indies
        Fax: (1) 869 469 1204

Please mark initial fax: Attn: New Client Department

About the Author

Adam Starchild is the author of over twenty books, and hundreds of magazine articles, primarily on business and finance. His articles have a appeared in a wide range of publications around the world — including *Business Credit, Euromoney, Finance, The Financial Planner, International Living, Offshore Financial Review, Reason, Tax Planning International, Trusts & Estates*, and many more.
His personal website on the Internet is at http://www.cyberhaven.com/starchild